THE CURIOUS
SHOPPER'S GUIDE TO
NEW YORK CITY

THE CURIOUS SHOPPER'S GUIDE TO

New York City

Inside Manhattan's Shopping Districts

BY PAMELA KEECH

The Little Bookroom • New York

Acknowledgements
The author thanks Angela Hederman and Nadia Aguiar of The Little Bookroom,
Lisa Kressbach, Meg Pinto, Nicholas Prince, April Sievert, Sheree Sievert,
Helene Silver, and especially all the merchants.

Second Printing December 2006
Printed in China

Published by The Little Bookroom
1755 Broadway, 5th floor
New York NY 10019
(212) 293-1643
fax (212) 333-5374
editorial@littlebookroom.com
www.littlebookroom.com

For the pushcart vendors, stitchers,
milliners, craftsmen, printers, traders, inventors,
and dreamers who started it all.

TABLE OF CONTENTS

INTRODUCTION

FOR ANYONE INTERESTED IN UNCOMMON RE-
TAIL, MANHATTAN IS A MECCA. IN NEW YORK
City there still are enclaves of independent merchants
devoted to specialty goods—items as diverse as flowers,
kitchenware, buttons, underwear, diamonds, light
fixtures, and musical instruments. The stores are clus-
tered in small areas, sometimes within one or two blocks,
and support each other for their own convenience and
that of their customers. Many of these stores have been
family owned for several generations, and a few are more
than a hundred years old. Some merchants who have
been selling to the trade only for decades have begun
to open their doors to the public, offering a plethora
of high-quality, unusual, and innovative merchandise,
much of it at discounted prices. The curious and intrepid
can seek out unique items that inspire the décor, clothing,

jewelry, music, cuisine, and parties of one of the greatest cities of the world.

Visiting a district for the first time can be overwhelming. Reactions may range from exhilaration at the Flower Market to complete bewilderment in the Diamond District. In this book I familiarize the shopper with the protocol for each district to help make an otherwise mystifying experience into a comfortable adventure. Each section begins with a historical introduction and some general advice, followed by a description of each selected store, and finally a few suggestions of where to eat along the route. Routes usually go up one side of the street and down the other. Restaurants are considered inexpensive if lunch for one without alcoholic beverages costs less than $10, moderate if up to $20, and expensive if over $20.

The stores listed are only a portion of those found in a district. I selected them for the variety of their stock, their hospitable atmosphere, and the integrity of their owners; those omitted may be just as interesting. There are some merchants who still sell to the trade only, and none of those is included in this book.

Manhattan real estate is always in a state of flux. Established stores, markets, and entire districts may move or close as property changes hands, and, regrettably, some of the stores listed here may be out of business by the time the book is published. It is my hope that the record made of them here will help preserve their legacy.

Pamela Keech
NEW YORK CITY

KITCHENWARE

BOWERY FROM DELANCEY TO BLEECKER STREETS

🚇 B, D TO GRAND STREET; J, M, Z TO BOWERY;

F, V TO SECOND AVENUE

THE BOWERY BETWEEN HOUSTON AND DELANCEY STREETS IS A BIG CLANKING DISTRICT OF more than thirty supply stores that service restaurants in all five boroughs and beyond. On both sides of the street, great stainless steel sinks flank entrances to stores filled with used industrial stoves and counters; there are always men outside hosing down yet more equipment to offer for sale. A dozen or so stores sell pots and pans, china, glassware, and kitchen utensils. The Bowery has been home to such places since the 1930s.

In the nineteenth century the Bowery sported saloons, music halls, pawnshops, dime museums (which always featured at least one mermaid`, burlesque houses, and beer gardens. Crowds flocked to see minstrel shows, flea circuses, organ grinders, cockfights, and glass-eaters like Bill "A piece of window glass between two slices of white bread is nice" Jones. In the first half of the twentieth century it became skid row, darkened by the Third Avenue El, lined with flophouses that provided a piece of canvas slung between two poles for a quarter a night.

Some old-timers say that restaurant supply stores settled in during the Depression because the hard-luck men who lived on the Bowery were cheap laborers willing to unload crates of dishes and heavy kitchen equipment. Some point out that the street's location, near the docks on the East River, was convenient. It is certain that the stores were there—twenty suppliers of restaurant equipment were listed on the Bowery in the 1939 Yellow Pages.

BOWERY RESTAURANT SUPPLY

183 BOWERY (AT DELANCEY STREET)

☎ 212 254 9720 · *www.boweryrestaurantsupply.com*

MON-FRI 9AM-6PM; SAT 9AM-5PM; CLOSED SUN

What to look for: diner-style china

BOWERY RESTAURANT SUPPLY IS IN THE FOR-MER PURITAN HOTEL, A FLOPHOUSE WHERE ONE could sleep for 40¢ a night. Now, sixty-some years later, a nifty set of salt and pepper shakers is just 10¢ more. Long shelves hold bins full of diner-style tableware—heavy white china coffee mugs sell for $1 each, and plastic tumblers are 65¢. All-but-unbreakable plates with vintage-inspired pink decorative edging are $2. Assorted kitchen utensils are under $3. Woks are available in an array of sizes, and you'll find a substantial assortment of inexpensive cooking pots, frying pans, and strainers. A package of ten sets of plastic chopsticks is $2.50; a set of

[17]

ten in bamboo is 40¢. The store also sells stainless steel furnishings, including worktables, shelving, cabinets, and special ovens for roasting ducks or pigs; individual specification sheets are on the website. Customization is possible. Delivery is available at an extra charge.

LEADER TRADING COMPANY

191 BOWERY (DELANCEY / RIVINGTON STREETS)

☎ 212 677 1982

MON-FRI 9AM-6PM; SAT 10AM-4PM; CLOSED SUN

What to look for: Asian tableware and cookware

LEADER CARRIES A PRODIGIOUS AMOUNT OF DIS-COUNTED CERAMIC AND LACQUERED ASIAN tableware, including soy sauce dishes, plates ($3-$6), rice and noodle bowls ($2-$6), chopstick rests, sake sets, and teapots. The graceful shapes of dishes—square, rectangular, round, triangular, and oval—and delicate colors and patterns allow for mixing and layering stylized place settings. For playful presentations of sushi and sashimi, two-foot laquered sushi boats start at $35; for grand occasions there are wooden boats three or more feet long, some with sails.

For the chef there are wooden sushi-oke mixing

bowls, sushi molds, aprons, and Japanese chef head-bands. The staff is patient and will help customers who are unsure of the function of or proper use for any items. Shipping is available.

ADVANCE KITCHEN SUPPLIES

193 BOWERY (DELANCEY/RIVINGTON STREETS)

☎ 212 674 1818

DAILY 9AM-5:30PM

What to look for: huge pots

THIS SITE WAS ONCE MILITARY HALL, AN ASSEM-
BLY SPACE FOR POLITICAL AND ORGANIZATIONAL
meetings. Here, in the 1840s, New York City policemen
first agreed to wear uniforms and in 1863 the tinsmiths
of New York founded the first sheet-metal workers union
in the country. In 1868 a group of actors and entertainers founded the Elks, and in 1892 the radical Emma
Goldman defended her lover's assassination attempt on
Henry Clay Frick.

The current tenant has the most complete line of
graduated-size cooking pots on the Bowery. The largest
holds twenty-five gallons.

BALTER SALES COMPANY

209 BOWERY (DELANCEY/RIVINGTON STREETS)

☎ 212 674 2960

MON-FRI 8AM-4PM; CLOSED SAT-SUN

What to look for: discounted designer tableware

THE UNASSUMING ENTRANCE TO BALTER (THROUGH THE LOADING DOCK, WITH THE SHOWROOM ENTrance door on the left) belies the gorgeous tableware sold by this upscale supplier. Glass and china plates in elegant contemporary shapes by Villeroy & Boch and Renol catch light from the windows, while reproduction Fiesta dinnerware provides background color to heavy hotel-style china made by Homer Laughlin, Syracuse China, Royal Doulton, and Corby Hall, among others. Many items are sold wholesale by the case only, but there is usually a large selection of loose discontinued items that are sold by the piece at below retail prices, and the

stock varies constantly. For parties and weddings, cases of champagne flutes, punch cups, and wine glasses are good investments. There is no website, but items can be ordered by phone or fax and shipped all over the world.

CHEF RESTAURANT SUPPLY

294-298 BOWERY (HOUSTON/BLEECKER STREETS)

☎ 212 254 6644

MON-SAT 9AM-5:30PM; SUN 11AM-4:30PM

What to look for: discounted high-end knives

COMPARISON SHOPPING REVEALS THAT CHEF SUPPLY MAY HAVE THE LOWEST PRICES IN THE district. Twelve-inch Myland anodized aluminum non-stick skillets are $22, and twelve-inch Lodge cast-iron skillets with opposing handles for easier lifting are $19.95. At the upper end, but still quite competitively priced, are eleven-inch Mauviel Cuprinox copper skillets at $141. Chef carries several well-regarded brands of knives in a range of prices. Among knives with eight-inch blades are Russell knives with plastic handles, $12.95; Mundial forged knives with tang, $19.95; and Zwilling J. A. Henckels, $50. A ten-inch Yanagiba is $51.95.

Miscellaneous items include granite mortar and pestle sets for $35, a variety of good-looking embossed chrome serving trays and platters for $3-$6, three-tiered stainless steel serving carts for $195, restaurant chairs for $50, and bamboo steamers from $2.95-$7.95. There are also chef's hats, jackets, aprons, and checked pants; butcher blocks and cutting boards; kitchen scales; blenders and mixers; and, for garnish, garlands of bright green plastic parsley.

KINCO

248 BOWERY (HOUSTON / PRINCE STREETS)

☎ 212 226 0709

MON-FRI 9AM-5PM; SAT 10AM-4PM; CLOSED SUN

What to look for: baking supplies

THIS SMALL, SHINY STORE CARRIES EVERY-
THING FOR THE PROFESSIONAL BAKESHOP
and the passionate home baker, and it has a working
model kitchen where baking techniques are demon-
strated. Owned by the Fung family, who also owns Leader
Trading, Kinco stocks a special line of professional-
quality baking pans made of hard-anodized aluminum
that conducts heat evenly but will not leach into food.
The home baker will also be interested in massive roll-
ing pins, mixing bowls, mixers, cookie cutters, chocolate
molds, heart-shaped cake pans, and cake rings and pie
trays in assorted sizes. For cake decorating there are pas-

try bags and tips, professional icing spatulas and combs, two- and three-tier cake stands, and eighteen-inch cake knives ($28.95). Wire and wicker baskets and trays for baked goods presented as gifts are $4-$8. Kinco also carries a selection of industrial-quality coffee- and cappuccino-makers at competitive prices.

BARI RESTAURANT & PIZZERIA EQUIPMENT CORP.

240 BOWERY (HOUSTON / PRINCE STREETS)

1 PRINCE STREET (AT BOWERY) ☎ 212 925 3845

MON-FRI 8AM-5PM; SAT 9AM-3PM; CLOSED SUN

What to look for: discounted pizza making supplies

GRANDLY OCCUPYING THE CENTER OF THE BLOCK SINCE 1950, THIS THIRD-GENERATION BUSINESS is named for the family's ancestral hometown in Italy. Equipment for pizza kitchens is a specialty, and Bari designs, builds, and installs pizza kitchens, as well as general restaurant, deli, and home kitchens. Bari recommends its line of small wood-burning pizza ovens for backyards. There are pasta machines, all sizes of pizza pans (including deep dish), pizza cutters, wooden pizza paddles, gleaming chafing dishes, colorful acrylic cutting boards, blenders, slicers, Bari's own line of pots and

[34]

pans, and a whimsical assortment of life-sized Italian restaurant display figures, all at prices well below retail. A satellite store at the corner of Bowery and Prince (#1) has restaurant tables and chairs.

MARKS RESTAURANT EQUIPMENT CO.

210 BOWERY (HOUSTON / PRINCE STREETS)

☎ 212 219 0200

MON-FRI 8AM-5PM; SAT 9AM-3PM; CLOSED SUN

What to look for: discounted unusual kitchen utensils

WALKING INTO MARKS IS LIKE WALKING INTO A MASSIVE KITCHEN THAT HAS BEEN BEDEVILED by poltergeists. There is absolutely everything one could possibly need, and it is strewn in all directions. The owner says the store has "all the tchotchkes in the world" and will sell wholesale or retail—the more you buy, the less it costs. There are scales, ladles, strainers, dippers, wire baskets, electric cheese grinders, food processors, blenders, conveyor toasters, and other machines whose functions are not immediately evident. Marks is particularly fun for those who like to dig for a bargain.

RESTAURANTS

FREEMANS
End of Freeman Alley off Rivington Street
(Bowery/Chrystie Street)
☎ 212 420 0012 · *www.freemansrestaurant.com*
Daily 5-11:30pm; Sat-Sun brunch 11am-3:30pm

Hidden restaurant at the end of one of New York's few alleys. Dining room has a hunting-lodge atmosphere. Not open for lunch. Serves weekend brunch, drinks, and early dinner at the end of a shopping day. American and Irish/English food. Moderate.

BLVD CAFÉ
BLVD RESTAURANT
199 Bowery (at Spring Street)
☎ 212 982 7767 · *www.blvdnyc.com*
Café: Mon-Sat 8am-4pm; Restaurant: Tue-Sun 6-11pm

Breakfast and light fare of sandwiches and salads during the day in the sunny café, Latin/Asian-themed dining in the restaurant, and a lounge and night club for drinks. Inexpensive to moderate.

THE KITCHEN CLUB
30 Prince Street (at Mott Street)
☎ 212 274 0025 · *www.thekitchenclub.com*
Lunch: Tue-Fri 12-3:30pm; Dinner: daily 5:30pm-11pm

Part Continental, part Japanese, part pure imagination. Dumplings filled with duck/ginger, tofu/chrysanthemum, chocolate. Smoked salmon, mascarpone, and cucumber sandwich, rare tuna with wasabi sauce. Moderate.

CONGEE BOWERY RESTAURANT AND BAR
207 Bowery (Delancey/Rivington Streets)
☎ 212 766 2828 · *www.congeevillage.com*
Daily 11am-2am

Cantonese theme park feel with fountain, koi pond, and bamboo trees. Specializes in congee, an ancient rice porridge (also called jook or juk in China) that is reputed to settle the stomach and digestive tract. Served thirty ways, including with crab, abalone and frog, and chicken with black mushrooms ($3.95). Additional lunch specials are $3.50-$4.95; inexpensive to moderate.

See also restaurant listings on page 69.

THE BOWERY
LIGHTING

THE BOWERY
LIGHTING

LIGHTING

BOWERY FROM GRAND TO DELANCEY STREETS

🚇 B, D TO GRAND STREET; J, M, Z TO BOWERY;

F, V TO SECOND AVENUE

IN THE NINETEENTH CENTURY THEATERS LINED THE BOWERY. AT THE ORIENTAL, THE THALIA, the People's, and other venues, Shakespeare and Ibsen were presented alternately with melodramas such as *The Girl I Left Behind Me*, *The Waifs of New York*, and *Tom Edison the Electrician*.

The lighting fixture trade began to settle on the lower end of the Bowery in part to support the needs of the area's many theaters, which required an extraordinary amount of luminescence for both the stage and the house. A typical theater used gas brackets backstage and as house lights; gas wings and border lights to surround the stage; and limelights—early spotlights that used gas to heat cones of limestone that became brilliantly incandescent—for the stage itself.

Savvy immigrants capitalized on the need by opening businesses that distributed, installed, and maintained theater lighting. They also served home lighting needs. One name still prominent in lighting, Lightolier, started on Bowery as the New York Gas Appliance Company in 1904. Today there are more than twenty-five stores in the district.

BOWERY LIGHTING

132 BOWERY (GRAND/BROOME STREETS)

☎ 212 941 3244

DAILY 9:30AM-6PM

What to look for: ornate chandeliers

Bowery Lighting is arranged gallery-style as a series of individual room settings that integrate classically inspired furniture with decorative European lighting. Somewhat plainer glass fixtures are displayed at the front of the store. Toward the rear the lights get bigger and gaudier, glass changes to metal, and finally to cherubs and entwined lovers that sit atop an enameled fixture with gilt arms and ornate shades. (That impressive chandelier is $12,499.) Adjoining the main room is a smaller room filled with chandeliers and pendants made of Austrian crystal.

SOVEREIGN LIGHTING

138 BOWERY (GRAND / BROOME STREETS)

☎ 212 966 5644 · *www.sovereignlighting.com*

DAILY 9:30AM-5:30PM

What to look for: discounted high-end lighting

SOVEREIGN SPECIALIZES IN DESIGNING TRACK, MONORAIL, AND RECESSED LIGHTING SYSTEMS. The staff consults a customer's floor plan to come up with the best solution for the best price. The variety of fixtures in stock are appropriate for a range of interior design styles; the Murano bowl chandeliers by LBL would add luster to any uptown Manhattan foyer, while the industrialesque sconces by Hi-Lite would be perfectly at home in a downtown loft. A nice variety of porch and yard lighting is available, as is the complete line of Hunter ceiling fans.

NEW GENERATION LIGHTING

144 BOWERY (GRAND/BROOME STREETS)

☎ 212 966 0328 · *www.newgenerationlighting.com*

MON-FRI 9:30AM-6:30PM; SAT-SUN 9:30AM-7PM

What to look for: contemporary minimalist lighting at wholesale prices

PAINTED SKY BLUE, AND FILLED WITH THE LIGHT OF MORE THAN A THOUSAND FIXTURES, NEW Generation's showroom has the ambience of a summer afternoon. Sleek, minimalist lighting is the specialty. Curvilinear chandeliers with multicolor bulbs hang from the ceiling. Glass pendants and colored globes float over torchieres and floor lamps. Two long walls are filled with spotlights, track fixtures, and sconces. Lamps include classic table lamps with drum shades, as well as novelty and children's styles; there is a wide array of task lighting as well. The store carries many designs

by Lite Source and other North American companies; three-quarters of the stock comes from manufacturers in California or Canada. All items are sold to the public at wholesale prices. Telephone orders are taken between 10am and 7pm. A personal shopping assistant is available to answer questions in person or by phone.

LIGHTING BY GREGORY

158 BOWERY (BROOME/DELANCEY STREETS)

☎ 212 226 1276 · *www.lightingbygregory.com*

DAILY 9AM-5:30PM

*What to look for: wide selection of styles by
well-known manufacturers*

THE LARGEST LIGHTING STORE ON THE BOW-
ERY, MILDLY CHAOTIC LIGHTING BY GREGORY
has been a mainstay of the district for twenty years,
carrying a huge selection of tasteful contemporary and
traditional lighting at discount prices. Lightolier, the
Modern Fan Company, and Kovacs are but a few of the
well-known brands filling the sixteen-thousand-square-
foot showroom that houses every imaginable variety of
chandelier, pendant, track, fixture, sconce, table lamp,
floor lamp, and ceiling fan (there are four categories
alone of ceiling fans: contemporary, traditional, transi-

tional, and outdoor). The full range of Lutron dimmers and switches is stocked, too. A consultant is available to help design indoor and outdoor lighting for homes, targeted lighting for art collections, and comprehensive lighting plans for retail stores, offices, restaurants, and hotels. A large warehouse means that goods are seldom out of stock. Many of the items can be ordered on the website. Price guarantees, shipping terms, and return policies are complex and are best consulted online.

OGGI LIGHTING

166 BOWERY (BROOME / DELANCEY STREETS)

☎ 212 226-6444 · *www.oggilighting.com*

DAILY 9:30AM-5PM

What to look for: high-style designs from Spain and Italy

THE SELECTION OF MODERN, TRADITIONAL, AND WHIMSICAL LIGHTING IMPORTED FROM EUROPE is original enough to provoke optical inspiration and restrained enough not to overwhelm. Most fixtures are from Spain and Italy and are of high quality and high style. An amusing line of hanging fixtures features vehicles—trains. helicopters, sailboats, motorcycles, airplanes—that could hover on the ceiling of any child's room. Stock can be viewed and ordered on the website. Bulbs are included at no charge, and shipping within the continental United States is free.

JUST SHADES

21 SPRING STREET (AT ELIZABETH STREET)

☎ 212 966 2757 · *www.justshadesny.com*

TUE-FRI 9:30-6:00; SAT 9:30-5:00; CLOSED SUN-MON

What to look for: trendy lampshades

JUST SHADES PROVIDES A VAST SELECTION OF IN-STOCK LAMPSHADES. TRADITIONAL AND CONtemporary styles are available in materials such as silk string, parchment, silk, linen, and paper. There are solids, stripes, and prints, as well as the standard white and ecru. Custom shades are available in any material; a variety of fabric is stocked to choose from, or customers can furnish their own. It is best to bring the lamp when ordering custom shades. Lampshades can be taken on approval. Stock shades range from about $12 to over $300. The website contains a diagram on how to measure for a shade.

[57]

LIGHTING CRAFTSMAN

173 BOWERY (AT DELANCEY STREET)

☎ 212 966 4474

MON-SAT 9:30AM-6:30PM; SUN 10:30AM-6:30PM

*What to look for: quirky industrial-look light fixtures,
Tiffany-style lamps*

THIS STORE STOCKS ONE OF THE LARGEST SEL-
ECTIONS OF TIFFANY-STYLE LAMPS ON THE EAST
Coast But don't be misled by the abundant stained
glass—Lighting Craftsman is a favorite of young Lower
East Side residents and the hip architects they use, who
are drawn to the in-house designed wall and ceiling fixtures, fabricated from industrial parts, and finished with
bronze and coppery patinas.

O'LAMPIA

155 BOWERY (AT BROOME STREET)
☎ 212 925 1660 · *www.olampia.com*
TUE-SUN 10AM-6PM; CLOSED MON
What to look for: custom light fixtures

KWANGSUNG LEE IS A PAINTER AND DESIGNER OF LIGHT FIXTURES AND LAMPS. HIS ORIGINAL concept was to design fixtures suitable for brownstone renovations, but the range of restrained and elegant pieces here would be appropriate in more contemporary settings as well. He makes updated versions of traditional early American lighting, and many of his creations are influenced by Shaker designs. All orders are custom made, handcrafted in Manhattan and Brooklyn, based on floor samples that can be ordered as is, smaller or larger, in any number of finishes, with a choice of shades and colors. Styles are pictured on the website.

[61]

BROOME LAMPSHADES

325 BROOME STREET (BOWERY/CHRYSTIE STREET)

☎ 212 431 9666 · *www.lampshadesny.com*

DAILY 9:30AM–6PM

What to look for: custom lampshades

BROOME LAMPSHADES SPECIALIZES IN THE FABRICATION OF HIGH-QUALITY CUSTOM LAMPSHADES. Frames are constructed on site and the turnaround is very quick—usually one to ten days. Customers can bring their own fabric or select from stock that includes fine silk and other high-end materials. Antique and vintage shades can be restored or recovered. The store also has a showroom of in-stock shades with American, European, and Asian sockets in many sizes, styles, and price ranges. Harps and a nice selection of decorative finials are also sold. It is best to bring the lamp if possible. Simple custom lampshades start at $40.

GOLT LIGHTING AND COOKWARE

163 BOWERY (GRAND/DELANCEY STREETS)

☎ 212 431 7308

DAILY 10AM-7PM

What to look for: fun lighting

AMONG THE PROLIFERATION OF ASIAN LIGHTING STORES ON THE BOWERY, GOLT'S WONDERfully kitschy inventory stands out. You'll find flashing multicolor concoctions, illuminated way-oversized floral displays, and six-foot metal palm trees with white lights running up and down the fronds. Fans of pyrotechnics will appreciate the Firework—a large hanging fixture that simulates a multicolored explosion. For the Chinese restaurant look (or an actual Chinese restaurant), check out the sparkling boat-shaped chandeliers in two sizes, small for the home and large for commercial settings. Aquariums are a sideline. The cookware is next door.

[65]

[66]

THE LIGHTING SHOWROOM

137 BOWERY (GRAND/DELANCEY STREETS)

☎ 212 431 3880

MON-SAT 10AM-5PM; CLOSED SUN

What to look for: lamps and sconces in the
Arts and Crafts style

THE SLIGHTLY DUSTY SHOWROOM HERE BRIMS WITH TRADITIONAL CHANDELIERS, TABLE AND floor lamps, and sconces, as well as modern fixtures.

The highlights of the collection are lamps handmade by two California companies that specialize in lighting influenced by the Arts and Crafts movement. The Mica Lamp Company reproduces the designs of early twentieth-century coppersmith Dirk Van Erp; lamps are made of solid copper with mica shades that produce a soft light. Another line, the whimsical Storybook collection, consists of hanging lanterns that look as if they're straight out of the Brothers Grimm. A second company, Arroyo Craftsmen, bases its simple lamps of brass and mica on the designs of Frank Lloyd Wright and Charles Rennie Mackintosh. All stock is priced at 50 percent off the manufacturer's suggested retail price.

IN BRIEF

BULBS WORLD
121-N Chrystie Street
(Broome / Grand Streets)
☎ 212 941 8265
Daily 9:30am-6pm

Lightbulbs—incandescent, halogen, spot, flood, chandelier, Christmas, and three styles of Edison bulbs with glowing filaments; extension cords; outlet adapters; track lighting fixtures; pendant lights; task lighting.

RESTAURANTS

ITALIAN FOOD CENTER
186 *Grand Street (at Mulberry Street)*
☎ 212 925 2954
Daily 8am-10pm

Self-service homemade Italian food, very casual atmosphere with small seating area. Pasta, hero sandwiches, calzones, fresh mozzarella. Inexpensive.

BARMARCHÉ
14 *Spring Street (Elizabeth/Mott Streets)*
☎ 212 219 2399 · *www.barmarche.com*
Mon-Wed 11am-midnight; Thu-Fri 11am-2am; Sat 9am-2am;
Sun 9am-midnight

Chic but unpretentious restaurant serving food influenced by Spanish, Mexican, and other global cuisines. Dishes include swordfish with crushed avocado, jalapeño, and crème fraîche; goat cheese brûlée with roasted beets; inventive cocktails. Moderate to expensive.

DUMPLING HOUSE

118A *Eldridge Street (Grand/Broome Streets)*

☎ 212 625 8008

Daily 7:30am-9:30pm

Chinese hole-in-the-wall touted by Marcella Hazan, among others. Five delicious dumplings for $1; hot and sour, wonton, or beef noodle soup (large size, $2). No seating.

See also the restaurant listings on page 38.

UNDERGARMENTS

ORCHARD STREET TO ESSEX STREET,

BETWEEN HOUSTON AND GRAND STREETS

🚊 F, V TO SECOND AVENUE

SINCE THE LATE NINETEENTH CENTURY, MAKING AND SELLING CLOTHING HAS BEEN PART OF LIFE on the Lower East Side—the original Garment District. Undergarments were big business; 10 to 20 percent of all underwear in the United States was made in the area. Entrepreneurial immigrants from Eastern Europe ran small sweatshops in 325-square-foot apartments, opened shops in tenement storefronts, or adopted pushcarts as a way to earn a living with minimal overhead. In 1930 there were forty-three underwear and hosiery dealers on Orchard Street. Some outlets were operated by great-grandparents of the merchants who still carry on their family businesses in the neighborhood.

While their fathers tended businesses, many immigrant girls worked as seamstresses at home or in factories. There was little room for advancement in the sewing lofts, but the corset business afforded one possible step up. Skilled corsetiers could make decent money, and as corsets evolved into brassieres during the early twentieth century, some women were able to become fitters or even inventors.

The first modern uplift brassiere was created in 1922 by a Russian immigrant seamstress, Ida Rosenthal, her sculptor husband William, and her partner Enid Bissett at their custom dress shop, Enid Frocks, on West 57th Street. Rosenthal, a full-figured woman, took exception to the fashionable boyish flapper figure: "Nature made women with a bosom, so why fight nature?" Their invention was a great success in the shop, and they soon began to manufacture their own brassieres. To counter a popular undergarment label of the day, Boyish Form, they christened their prototype Maiden Form.

A foray into the underwear stores of the Lower East Side can be unnerving. Most of the stores are quite small, and many have not redecorated in forty or more years, if they were ever decorated at all. Merchandise displays may consist solely of teetering piles of boxes with cryptic style and size numbers written on the ends. The lighting is sometimes feeble, and male proprietors can be intimidating. But there are good reasons to go— the stores carry a huge selection of styles at discounted prices and offer many sizes that are impossible to find elsewhere. And the staffs give personalized service that cannot be equaled in department or specialty stores.

ORCHARD CORSET
DISCOUNT CENTER

157 ORCHARD STREET

(STANTON / RIVINGTON STREETS)

☎ 212 674 0786 · 877 267 2427 · *www.orchardcorset.com*

SUN–THU 10AM–6PM; FRI 10AM–3PM; CLOSED SAT

What to look for· bra fitting, hard-to-find sizes at discounted prices

WITHOUT FRILLS BUT PLENTIFULLY STOCKED, ORCHARD CORSET DISCOUNT CENTER HAS been in business since the 1930s. The current owners took over in 1968, inspired by matriarch Magda Bergstein's long experience in the industry. It is the best place to be fitted. The bewildering jumble of boxes on the floor-to-ceiling shelves is no puzzle for the supremely professional female staff who, behind two curtains hung on strings, take all the time necessary to ensure that fit

and style are perfect for the individual figure, from size 32-56 A-J cups.

Orchard Corset also sells girdles, waist-cinchers, slips, panties, undershirts, and thermal underwear by manufacturers that include Va Bien, Tatiana, and Annette. A good selection of bridal corsets is offered, as well as strapped and strapless corsets adapted from classic Renaissance and Victorian styles. These are designed in-house and are available in white or colored damask satin and trimmed with flat braid. A new line consists of sheer, colored chemise tops and panties. The package price for the chemise, panties, and a corset is less than $100. Items can be ordered on the website.

MAJESTIC LINGERIE

86 ORCHARD STREET (BROOME / GRAND STREETS)

☎ 212 473 7990 · *www.majesticlingerie.com*

SUN-THU 9AM-5:30PM; FRI 9AM-TWO HOURS

BEFORE SUNSET; CLOSED SAT

What to look for: hard-to-find sizes at discounted prices

WHEN ASKED WHO WEARS GIRDLES THESE DAYS, MAJESTIC'S OWNER REPLIED, "EVERYBODY— women's great wish is to tuck their tummies." Majestic carries an array of girdle styles in sizes from small to 9X, and panties up to size 15 that can be bought in bulk for as low as $18 a dozen. Majestic also has its own line, Soprano, the "Golden Note in Lingerie," which was founded as a hosiery label in 1945 and now includes a full line of foundation garments, lingerie, sleepwear, and loungewear to size 3X. Other items include baby dolls, slips, robes, housedresses, hosiery, and knitwear in brands

including Berlina, Goddess, Nancy King, Bali, and Exquisite Form, as well as training and maternity bras. Merchandise can be viewed and ordered on the website.

HOWARD SPORTSWEAR, INC.

69 ORCHARD STREET (BROOME / GRAND STREETS)

☎ 212 226 4307 · 888 974 2727

www.shopatshellys.com

SUN-FRI 9AM-5:30PM; CLOSED SAT

What to look for: discounted men's underwear

IN A DISTRICT THAT FOCUSES ON LINGERIE FOR WOMEN, HOWARD'S STOCK OF MEN'S UNDERGARMENTS is a welcome anomaly. The store originally sold only men's underwear, adding women's and children's later. Today Howard's carries men's socks, pajamas, Jockey and Munsingwear shorts, T-shirts, and activewear. For women the inventory includes bras by Wacoal, Olga, Lilyette, Teenform, Nancy Ganz, and Chantelle. In the hip and tummy control department there are seriously controlling Rago girdles and more forgiving Flexees girdles. Berkshire maternity pantyhose and Morgan

thermal underwear are useful, as is a complete line of Danskin leotards, tights, ankle pants, and capris. Everything is sold below retail. There is free domestic shipping on orders over $50, and a thirty-day return policy.

A.W. KAUFMAN

73 ORCHARD STREET (BROOME / GRAND STREETS)

☎ 212 226 1629 · *www.awkaufman.com*

SUN-THU 10:30AM-5PM; FRI 10:30AM-2PM;

CLOSED SAT

What to look for: discounted high-end European lingerie

AT A. W. KAUFMANN THE PROPRIETOR IS THIRD-GENERATION, AND SO ARE SOME OF HER CUS-tomers. Women whose grandmothers shopped here for the finest imported lingerie still come to buy high-end, luxurious European- and American-made robes, night-gowns, and undergarments for women and cashmere and silk robes for men. The store is overflowing with merchandise. As is still is the custom on the street, this store is not self-service but the staff is extremely wel-coming and helpful. Orders are taken by phone or fax and shipped promptly.

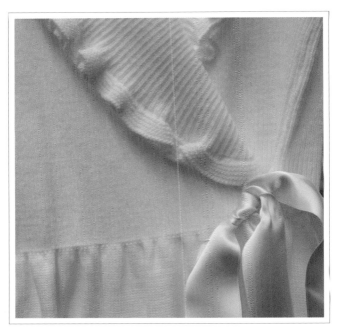

AMERICAN INTIMATES INTERNATIONAL

326 GRAND STREET (ORCHARD / LUDLOW STREETS)

☎ 212 674 2299 · *www.americanintimates.com*

CALL FOR HOURS

*What to look for: discounted undergarments;
extensive website*

OWNER JACK MINTZ SEEMS DELIGHTED AND A BIT SURPRISED WHEN CUSTOMERS ENTER HIS tiny shop, probably because much of his business is done on his website, which is the most comprehensive and easily navigated of all the neighborhood stores' sites. He carries off-price brand name underwear for men, women, and children. Some orders may qualify for free shipping, and there is a thirty-day return policy.

ISAAC SULTAN & SONS

330 GRAND STREET (ORCHARD/LUDLOW STREETS)

☎ 800 999 1645 · *www.isaacsultan.com*

MON-THU 9:15AM-5PM; FRI 9:15AM-2PM;

SUN 9AM-1PM; CLOSED SAT

What to look for: undergarments for those with special needs

THE SULTAN FAMILY HAS BEEN SELLING WOMEN'S UNDERGARMENTS FOR MORE THAN THIRTY years, specializing in hard-to-find styles and sizes for extraordinary figures, from 32DDD to 48H. The store is particularly good at supplying comparable foundation garments to older customers whose favorite styles are no longer made, and furnishing support garments that address a variety of medical conditions. Much business is now done on the website, where prices are 20 percent less than retail; store discounts can be even greater.

[91]

RESTAURANTS

KATZ'S DELICATESSEN
205 East Houston Street (at Ludlow Street)
☎ 212 254 2246 · 800 4HOTDOG · *www.katzdeli.com*
Sun-Tue 8am-10pm; Wed 8am-11pm; Thu 8am-midnight;
Fri-Sat 8am-3am

The Lower East Side's most famous delicatessen. Enormous pastrami and corned beef sandwiches, hot dogs; breakfast. Inexpensive to moderate.

RUSS & DAUGHTERS
179 E. Houston Street (Allen/Orchard Streets)
☎ 212 475 4880 · 800 RUSS 229 · *www.russanddaughters.com*
Mon-Sat 9am-7pm; Sun 8am-5:30pm

Some of the best caviar, including orange salmon roe, and smoked fish in New York City. Also fresh bagels, cheeses, herring, whitefish salad, halvah, rugelach, honey-roasted pecans, and hand-dipped chocolates. Take-out only; an "instant picnic" basket lunch is offered. Website offers full-service ordering. Inexpensive to moderate.

GUSS' PICKLES

85-87 Orchard Street (Broome / Grand Streets)

☎ 917 701 4000 · 800 620 GUSS · *www.gusspickle.com*

Tue-Thu & Sun 11am-5pm; Fri 9am-3pm; closed Sat, Mon

Kosher sour pickles, half-sour pickles, hot pickles, pickled tomatoes, sauerkraut, mushrooms, hot cherry peppers, and olives stuffed with almonds sold out of barrels on the street. Two pickles for $1; Guss' Pickles T-shirt $25. Can be ordered on the website, but more fun to eat on the street. Inexpensive.

BABYCAKES

248 Broome Street (Orchard / Ludlow Streets)

☎ 212 677 5047 · *www.babycakesnyc.com*

Tue-Thu 10am-10pm; Fri-Sat 10am-11pm;
Sun 10am-8pm; closed Mon

Scrumptious cakes, cupcakes, and cookies baked without refined sugar, gluten, wheat, dairy or nuts. Coffee and tea. Web orders taken. Inexpensive.

See also the restaurant listings on page 116.

DRAPERY & UPHOLSTERY FABRICS

DRAPERY & UPHOLSTERY FABRICS

DELANCEY TO GRAND STREETS, BETWEEN

FORSYTH AND ORCHARD STREETS

🚇 B, D TO GRAND STREET

EVEN BEFORE THE CIVIL WAR, IMPORTANT RETAILERS HAD ESTABLISHED FLAGSHIP STORES along Grand Street near Allen Street, and the area was a destination shopping district. Lord and Taylor opened a "fashion emporium" in 1853 at Grand and Chrystie Streets. Its competitor, Ridley's Department Store, was one of the largest stores of its day, and by 1886 it occupied the entire block of Grand from Allen to Orchard Streets, with adjoining stables in the rear providing parking for horses and carriages.

Immigrants who settled in the surrounding tenements were awed by the abundance of goods available just around the corner. They identified shopping with being an American and, having brought few worldly goods from the old country, became avid consumers. By the turn of the century a "tenement style" of decoration had evolved—a combination of printed fabrics, wallpapers, linoleums, and rugs. Mantels were draped with chintz, lace curtains hung at windows, and tables were covered with embroidered silk cloths. Pushcarts loaded with bolts of cloth, linens, tea sets, and fringed lamps took the place of the department stores that had since moved uptown. Between the wars the Grand Street area became a center of discounted curtains, upholstery goods and bedding (on Allen Street between Stanton and Grand, the bed linen district was advertised by colored quilts hung from poles). The reputation is upheld in the historic shops that remain.

At the discount fabric stores listed, price reductions may vary substantially depending on the amount of fabric bought, how long it has been in the store's inventory, the amount that remains on the bolt, and sometimes the whim of the owner. Some stores close in the early afternoon on Friday and are closed all day Saturday in observance of the Jewish Sabbath.

HARRIS LEVY

98 FORSYTH STREET (GRAND/BROOME STREETS)
☎ 212 226 3102 · 800 221 7750 · *www.harrislevy.com*
SUN-FRI 9AM-5PM; CLOSED SAT
What to look for: discounted high-end linens

IN 1894, HARRIS AND ESTHER LEVY CAME TO AMERICA FROM EASTERN EUROPE AND RENTED a pushcart to sell piece goods to immigrant women who sewed their own sheets. They were so successful that, in spite of the Depression, they purchased a lot on Grand Street in the early 1930s and erected the building their business still occupies. Now owned by the Levys' great-grandson and his wife, the store has been recently renovated but retains its period details of polychrome tin ceilings and exposed brick walls.

Italian and French sheets and coverlets by Sferra, Yves Delorme, and Bellino are sold at competitive prices.

[100]

You'll also find luxurious terry-cloth robes, silk lingerie, and cashmere throws. New additions are fine soaps, oils, and skin care products, including Ahava items from Israel and the Jack Black line of shaving products for men. Table linens are also stocked.

M & A DECORATORS

294 GRAND STREET (ELDRIDGE / ALLEN STREETS)

☎ 212 226 3910

SUN-THU 9:30AM-6PM; FRI 9:30AM-5PM;

CLOSED SAT

What to look for: discounted drapery fabric

M & A CATERS TO A RANGE OF CLIENTELE, FROM THE WELL-TO-DO TO NEWLYWEDS ON A BUD-get. This family-owned store is filled with a manageable selection of upholstery and drapery fabrics, including velvets, brocades, tapestries, and cottons, some as low as $5 per yard. Services offered include the fabrication of custom draperies, slipcovers, and upholstery.

ZARIN FABRICS &
HOME FURNISHINGS

314-318 GRAND STREET (AT ALLEN STREET)

☎ 212 925 6112 · *www.zarinfabrics.com*

SUN-FRI 9AM-6PM; SAT 10AM-6PM

What to look for: high-end designer fabrics

ROBERT ZARIN USED TO STAND ON A MILK CRATE TO SELL FABRIC FROM THE RACK IN FRONT OF his father Harry's original store on Orchard Street. Now he and his wife operate the largest of the discount design stores in the district, a one-stop paradise for both professional and DIY decorators. An impressive showroom on street level showcases furniture from a range of manufacturers, some at a substantial discount. Accessories include lamps, throw pillows, draperies, and vases.

The immense second floor loft is filled with floor-to-ceiling racks holding bolts of upholstery and drapery

[105]

fabrics that are organized by color and easily transported to the showroom for trial on a prospective sofa or chair. Manufacturers whose fabrics are regularly in stock include Kravat, Schumacher, Lee Jofa, and Laura Ashley. Fabrics can be viewed on the website by color or type of fabric; up to six swatches can be ordered for ninety-nine cents each. Free shipping is offered on larger orders. Interior design, custom upholstery, and drapery services are available.

BZI, INC.

314 GRAND STREET, LOWER LEVEL

(AT ALLEN STREET)

☎ 212 966 6690 · *www.zarinfabrics.com*

SUN-FRI 9AM-6PM; SAT 10AM-6PM

*What to look for: upholstering supplies
and drapery hardware*

ON THE LOWER LEVEL OF ZARIN FABRICS, BZI STOCKS UPHOLSTERING SUPPLIES, DRAPERY HARDWARE, ready-made drapery panels, decorative trimmings, and tiebacks. Necessities for upholstery—including webbing, burlap, staples, and tacks—are on hand. Custom drapery tracks can be cut to size and curved to specification.

MODERN DÉCOR

319 GRAND STREET (ALLEN / ORCHARD STREETS)

☎ 212 965 9240

SUN-THU 10AM-5:30PM; FRI BY APPOINTMENT;

CLOSED SAT

What to look for: closeout upholstery and drapery fabrics

THE OWNERS OF MODERN DÉCOR SAY THE PROFIT MARGIN ON THEIR FABRICS IS FLEXIBLE: "Sometimes we make a quarter, sometimes we make a dollar, but we don't let the customers leave empty-handed." They offer closeout upholstery and drapery fabrics, including embroidered raw silks, velvets, and cottons, starting at $4-6 per yard, as well as fringed and tasseled trims and tiebacks.

[109]

SHEILA'S DECORATING AND DESIGN EMPORIUM

68 ORCHARD STREET (GRAND/BROOME STREETS)

☎ 212 777 3767 · *www.sheilasdecorating.com*

SUN-THU 9AM-5PM; FRI 9AM-3PM; CLOSED SAT

What to look for: wallpaper

TRIMMINGS AND TASSELS SPILL OFF TABLES, AND WALLPAPER BOOKS TUMBLE OFF SHELVES as customers search for elements to create the perfect room. A long counter with stools provides a place to peruse samples. Two walls display bolts of domestic and imported designer fabrics, all sold at discount. A bargain basement offers fabrics and rolls of wallpaper at even lower prices (some as low as $10 per roll). Decorating services are available. Sheila's can fabricate upholstery, headboards, draperies, window treatments, tables, chairs, sofas, lamps, and bookcases.

JOE'S FABRIC WAREHOUSE

102-110 ORCHARD STREET (AT DELANCEY STREET)

☎ 212 674 7089

SUN-THU 9AM-6PM; FRI 9AM-3PM; CLOSED SAT

What to look for: discounted designer fabrics

THIS STORE HOLDS AN EXPANSIVE INVENTORY OF DECORATOR TEXTILES, ALL AT A RANGE OF discounted prices. Trimmings and tassels are displayed on the lower and street levels. A separate entrance leads to the second floor, which houses imported and domestic designer upholstery and drapery fabrics. The shop is usually crowded with film and theater designers and interior decorators. An expedition through the forest of upright bolts always yields rich finds from the constantly revolving stock. Joe's offers upholstery and window treatment services, and will send an interior designer to the homes of customers who desire expert decorating advice.

ECONOMY FOAM AND FUTONS

175 EAST HOUSTON STREET (AT ALLEN STREET)

☎ 212 473 4462 · *www.economyfoamandfutons.com*

TUE-FRI 9AM-6PM; SAT 11AM-6PM; SUN 10AM-5PM;

CLOSED MON

What to look for: pillow and cushion inserts

ECONOMY, IN BUSINESS SINCE 1937, IS ONE OF THE LARGEST FOAM CENTERS IN THE TRI-STATE AREA. It is a dependable source with a vast stock and discounted prices. Upholstery foam for cushions and mattresses can be cut while you wait. All densities of foam are available, as are a full range of standard sizes of inserts for throw pillows. Soundproofing foam is also available. Batting is sold by the yard and loose by the bag. The sleep department stocks Tempur-Pedic mattresses and pillows, foam mattresses, platform beds, and futons and frames. Fabrics and vinyl are sidelines. Delivery is available.

RESTAURANTS

88 ORCHARD STREET
88 Orchard Street (at Broome Street)
☎ 212 228 8880
Mon-Thu 7:30am-11pm; Fri 7:30am-11:30pm;
Sat 11:30am-8:30pm; Sun 8:30am-11pm

Freshly made sandwiches, salads, smoothies, and desserts in a casual setting. Iced coffee is served with coffee ice cubes for extra flavor. Inexpensive.

IL LABORATORIO DEL GELATO
95 Orchard Street (Broome/Delancey Streets)
☎ 212 343 9922 · *www.laboratoriodelgelato.com*
Daily 10am-6pm

Divine gelato and sorbet by the cone or cup in unusual flavors (bourbon pecan, tarragon with pink pepper, honey lavender, black mission fig, Concord grape, and champagne). Inexpensive.

'INOTECA

98 Rivington Street (at Ludlow Street)
☎ 212 614 0473 · *www.inotecanyc.com*
Daily noon-3am

Rustic wine bar with large selection of Italian wines and traditional small-plate dishes—antipasti, salads, salumi, cheeses, panini, and porchetta (roast suckling pig with herbs) sandwiches. Moderate.

EL CASTILLO DE JAGUA

113 Rivington Street (at Essex Street)
☎ 212 982 6412
Daily 8am-midnight

Established Dominican restaurant with homey vintage kitchen atmosphere. Fresh home-cooked food, large plates of roast meats with rice and beans, cod, ribs. Perfect pressed Cuban sandwich (roast pork, ham, cheese, pickle) for $3.50. Inexpensive.

See also the restaurant listings on page 92.

ART SUPPLIES & STATIONERY

THE AREA SURROUNDING THE FLATIRON BUILD-ING AT 23RD STREET AND FIFTH AVENUE HAS been variously called the Flatiron District, Chelsea, Midtown South, Ladies' Mile, the Photo District, and the Printing District.

In the second half of the nineteenth century a phalanx of magnificent cast-iron buildings was built along Broadway and Sixth Avenue from 9th to 23rd Streets, flanking the affluent brownstone residences along Fifth Avenue. Home to A. T. Stewart, R. H. Macy, B. Altman, and Siegel-Cooper Dry Goods, among others, the buildings created a shopping area called Fashion Row, which later became known as Ladies' Mile. The buildings are now home to specialty and chain stores.

Before digital printing processes made it unnecessary for printers to be physically near customers, printers followed their business, and the giant emporiums in Ladies' Mile were big business. Advertising signs, trade cards, price tags, sale notices, and handbills needed to be produced, with paper samples, typefaces, plates, and proofs carried between the printer and the client. Side streets on the east side of Sixth Avenue gradually filled with printers and printing-related businesses, including stationery shops, booksellers, and photographic supply and processing stores. The paper, art, and graphics supply shops and small printing businesses there continue to thrive today.

A. I. FRIEDMAN

44 WEST 18TH STREET (FIFTH / SIXTH AVENUES)

☎ 212 243 9000 · *www.aifriedman.com*

MON- FRI 9AM- 7PM; SAT 10AM- 7PM;

SUN 11AM- 6PM

What to look for: art supplies and journals

FRIEDMAN OFFERS A COMPREHENSIVE INVEN- TORY OF DISTINCTIVE SUPPLIES FOR ARTISTS, architects, and graphic designers—pencils, pastels, markers, brushes, canvas by the yard, stretchers, pre-stretched canvas, canvas boards, matte board, foam core, museum board, sketchbooks, as well as drafting tools and supplies and much, much more. Paints include Williamsburg Handmade Oil Colors, fine paints in unusual colors made in New York that are a favorite of leading contemporary artists. Custom framing is offered, as are ready-made picture frames.

For writers and archivers there are unusual journals, with polished hardwood covers and leather spines, by the Italian company Eccolo; elegant leather-bound albums by Raika; and handmade wedding and photo albums covered in raw silk by Rag & Bone. Moleskine notebooks in a variety of sizes and styles are always in stock. Business people will appreciate the comprehensive assortment of Filofax products; the stock of attaché cases and computer and tote bags; and stylish pens, business card cases, wallets, and watches by Acme Writing Tools (based on designs by Charles and Ray Eames, Antonio Gaudi, and Charles Rennie Mackintosh, among others). The extensive mail-order department can be accessed on the website or by telephone.

PAPER PRESENTATION

23 WEST 18TH STREET (FIFTH / SIXTH AVENUES)

☎ 212 463 7035 · *www.paperpresentation.com*

MON - FRI 9AM - 7PM; SAT 11AM - 6PM;

SUN NOON - 6PM

What to look for: stationery and printable invitations

SINCE 1991, PAPER PRESENTATION (FORMERLY PAPER ACCESS) HAS BEEN A DEPENDABLE SOURCE FOR A huge selection of stationery, résumé paper, and envelopes with a seemingly endless variety of basic and specialty text and cover stock in different colors and weights. Black liner, metallic, and lace paper are some of the more adventurous selections. The collection of invitations for ink-jet and laser printers includes designs by Vera Wang and Borghese; clever window, portfolio, saddle, and ribbon-tie styles; fold-over and shaped cards; and seal-and-send stock that becomes its own envelope.

The store has recently added a crafts department that is particularly strong in scrapbooking supplies, one of the first departments of its kind in New York City and certainly one of the most extensive, with albums, accordion book kits, adhesives, stickers, colored tags, and stencils. Other items include wrapping paper, seasonal cards and gifts, boxed notes, picture frames, pens, pencils, sealing wax, keepsake boxes, party favors, place cards, festive paper plates and napkins, sketchbooks, and presentation folders. You'll find blank award certificates in assorted colors, and metallic stick-on notarial seals. It is possible to order online; a catalog will be sent on request.

PRINTICON

7 WEST 18TH STREET (FIFTH/SIXTH AVENUES)

☎ 212 255 4489 · 866 PRINTICON · *www.printicon.com*

MON-FRI 8AM-8PM; SAT-SUN 11AM-6PM

*What to look for: high-end printing of
business cards and invitations*

FROM ITS UP-TO-THE-NANOSECOND MACINTOSH-
AND PC-POWERED DESIGN STUDIO TO ITS AN-
tique hand-operated letterpress machines, PrintIcon
offers full-service printing for business and social needs.
A favorite with corporate clients and advertising agen-
cies, the expansive store stocks a vast variety of fine
paper and card stock. A professional graphics and printing staff assists the customer through each step of
design and production. Services offered include printing of business cards, brochures, invitations, stationery,
holiday cards, presentation materials, banners, posters,

Where ...ets fine papers, anything is possible...

[129]

blueprints, laser prints, and iris prints. Elegant letterpress business cards cost $500-$1000 per five hundred and take about ten days to complete. For those who wish to design their own documents, templates are provided for download; papers and blank invitations can be purchased on the website.

SAM FLAX

12 WEST 20TH STREET (FIFTH/SIXTH AVENUES)

☎ 212 620 3000 · *www.samflax.com*

MON-FRI 9AM-7PM; SAT 10AM-6PM;

SUN NOON-6PM

What to look for: presentation binders and supplies;
office furniture

S AM FLAX WAS AN IMMIGRANT FROM EASTERN
EUROPE WHO STARTED SELLING ART SUPPLIES
from a pushcart in 1920. His business still sells art supplies but now specializes in high-design presentation
materials and office furniture. Everything for impressive presentations is available—brightly colored "padfo-
lios" by Alicia Klein; black folders for artwork by Itoya;
slick translucent and bookcase portfolios by Pina Zan-
garo, binders, boxes, and cases by Prat; gusseted folios in
alligator by Raika. Sam Flax also offers every size and

style of archival slide, photo, and CD protector; for storage and organization there is a comprehensive selection of archival storage boxes and supplies by Lineco. In the portables department there are stylish computer folders by Tucano, computer cases both hard and soft, and beautiful backpacks in many sizes.

Office furnishings include desks and drafting tables; chairs by Eames, Covey & Nelson, Eurostyle, Girsberger, and others; fashionable lighting; file cabinets in a range of colors; bookcases; and a plethora of well-designed desk accessories. Many items can be ordered online and shipped. Some furniture may need assembly.

TALAS

20 WEST 20TH STREET, FIFTH FLOOR

(FIFTH / SIXTH AVENUES)

☎ 212 219 0770 · *www.talasonline.com*

MON - FRI 9AM - 5:30PM

*What to look for: bookbinding supplies,
conservation materials*

TALAS CATERS TO THREE SPECIFIC AREAS—BOOK-
BINDING AND BOOK REPAIR, CONSERVATION AND
preservation, and custom presentation boxes and folders. The store carries very special supplies and tools
for making books and presentation folders, including a
remarkable selection of book cloth, leather, parchment,
vellum, and English and Italian marbleized endpaper.
Tools include bone, horn, and Teflon folding knives,
shears, linen tape, thread, needles, awls, push drills, drive
punches, glues, and flat glue brushes. For repair and

[135]

conservation professionals Talas carries chemicals and deacidifiers, lab safety supplies, restoration paints, gilding materials, cleaning and polishing supplies, archival storage supplies, and more. Talas makes by hand exquisite folios, presentation boxes, and keepsake boxes for individual and corporate clients. Boxes can be ordered in any size and covered in fine leather or other materials, and they can be partitioned and lined to specification. Hobbyists will appreciate kits that contain the basics for book repair, gilding, and storage of textiles; there is also a section of how-to books. Frames and framing supplies are also stocked.

Most items are available on the website. A complete catalog can be downloaded. The minimum purchase for shipping is $9; $9.50 for rolled items. Hazardous materials are charged a $30 handling fee per material.

RESTAURANTS

CITY BAKERY
3 West 18th Street (Fifth/Sixth Avenues)
☎ 212 366-1414 · *www.thecitybakery.com*
Mon-Fri 7:30am-7pm; Sat 7:30am-6:30pm; Sun 9am-6pm

Awards for the best salad bar, Buffalo wings, brunch, brownie, veggies, and all-American snack. Pretzel croissants are famous. Inexpensive to moderate.

CRAFTBAR
900 Broadway (19th/20th Streets)
☎ 212 461-4300 · *www.craftrestaurant.com/craftbar.html*
Lunch: Mon-Fri noon-2:30pm
Dinner: Sun-Mon 5:30-10pm; Tue-Sat 5:30-11pm

Italian-influenced appetizers and snacks. Moderate to expensive.

ALEO
7 West 20th Street (Fifth/Sixth Avenues)
☎ 212 691 8136 · *www.aleorestaurant.com*
Mon-Thu noon-11pm; Fri-Sat 12:30pm-midnight; Sun 4-10pm

Casual Mediterranean/Italian. Antipasti, panini, and salads served at lunch and at the bar. Known for romantic garden. Moderate.

ANTIQUES, COLLECTIBLES & VINTAGE STORES

CHELSEA, WHICH WAS NAMED FOR A SOLDIERS' HOME IN LONDON, THE ROYAL HOSPITAL CHELSEA, began as a rural neighborhood and was later populated by Irish Catholic immigrants. The history of the area is one of mixed usage. After the Civil War, William Marcy "Boss" Tweed made the area into a profitable center for vice that became known as The Tenderloin. In 1885 one-half of all buildings were reputed to house illegal activities.

In about 1910, loft buildings began to replace boardinghouses, flophouses, and brothels. Large department stores were constructed along Sixth Avenue, and the Flower District extended from 24th Street to 29th Street on both sides of Sixth Avenue. The Fur District was just west of Sixth Avenue in the Twenties. Early film production studios were located on 26th Street west of Seventh Avenue; Mary Pickford made *Tess of the Storm Country* (1914) in an old armory on West 26th Street. Light industry, printing companies, stores that sold industrial sewing machines, and Samuel French Dramatics Company (still there) were among some of the other enterprises.

THUNDER BAY ANTIQUES, LTD.

134 WEST 24TH STREET

(SIXTH / SEVENTH AVENUES)

☎ 212 633 8138 · *www.thunderbayltd.com*

TUE-SUN 11AM-7PM; CLOSED MON

What to look for: Asian and Middle Eastern antiques

THUNDER BAY IS FILLED WITH IDIOSYNCRATIC ANTIQUES, MANY FROM ASIA. YOU'LL FIND GOLDEN Buddhas, painted tables, and benches from Rajasthan, cabinets from Indonesia, daybeds from China, and armoires from Morocco, in addition to an occasional early American or Federal piece. A popular new line, Thunder Barn Ltd., is custom furniture made in upstate New York from wood salvaged from old barns. In-house design, refinishing, and restoration services are offered. Antique items are pictured, and can be ordered, on the website; catalog is also available. Domestic shipping is free.

[143]

OLDE GOOD THINGS

124 WEST 24TH STREET

(SIXTH / SEVENTH AVENUES)

☎ 212 989 8401 · *www.oldegoodthings.com*

DAILY 9AM-7PM

What to look for: architectural antiques

THE "ARCHITECTUROLOGISTS" (AS THE STAFF MEMBERS CALL THEMSELVES) AT OLDE GOOD THINGS follow wrecking balls all over North and South America in pursuit of architectural antiques. The 24th Street store has four levels filled with chandeliers, balustrades, lock sets, sinks, faucets, doors, windows, desks, statues, display cabinets, and much more. From an impossibly heavy sixteenth-century limestone mantel found in a Connecticut mansion to a sweet one-inch lock plate from the Plaza Hotel, the store displays a vast array of artifacts, including stained glass pieces and chestnut flooring—two cat-

egories that are increasingly difficult to find.

The firm has stores in multiple locations and a huge central warehouse in Scranton, Pennsylvania. More than two thousand items are available on the website. Prices are not always firm; some items have a "make an offer" button. There is a ten-day return policy.

THIS 'N' THAT COLLECTABLES

124 WEST 25TH STREET

(SIXTH / SEVENTH AVENUES)

☏ 212 255 0727 · *www.thisnthat-rey.com*

DAILY 10AM–6PM

What to look for: vintage costume jewelry

THE BAKELITE IN THE WINDOW OF THIS 'N' THAT IS ENOUGH TO WEAKEN THE KNEES OF THE MOST seasoned collector of vintage costume jewelry. The highly sought-after early plastic was invented in New York City in 1907 by a Belgian chemist, Dr. Leo Baekeland. It was used to make bracelets, flatware handles, and radio cases. It also was used, less familiarly, for the distributor head and cap in the Model A Ford, for the floor beneath the dancing feet of Fred Astaire and Ginger Rogers in the film *Top Hat*, and, experimentally, for lightweight coffins during World War II.

Anita Stern, the owner of This 'n' That, has been collecting Bakelite jewelry since the 1950s, when she was a teenager and bought it at Woolworth's. She also offers a dazzling array of vintage designer pieces by Trifari, Schiaparelli, Ciner, Miriam Haskell, and Coro, and contemporary designer pieces by Laura Carlillo, Barbera, and Lawrence Vrba. The shop glitters with thousands of crystals and rhinestones, Lucite and Bakelite necklaces are heaped on mannequins, and stacks of cases hold jewelry categorized by color, material, or motif.

Stern is a prized resource for designers, and she rents many of her pieces to stylists for print ads, editorial photographs, and films. Her jewelry is regularly seen adorning models in *Vogue, Elle, W, the London Times,* and *Harper's Bazaar.* In addition to jewelry you'll find vintage compacts, glassware, perfume bottles, lamps, chandeliers, and other period bric-a-brac. Shipping is available.

DECO ETC.

122 WEST 25TH STREET

(SIXTH / SEVENTH AVENUES)

☎ 212 675 3326

DAILY 11AM–6PM

What to look for: stylized lamps and Lucite handbags

DECO ETC. IS A MINI-MUSEUM OF MID-TWENTIETH-CENTURY INDUSTRIAL DESIGN. AT EACH TURN another pair of wildly imaginative lamps, a piece of streamlined furniture, or a quirky handbag comes into view. The shopwindow holds sculptural glass lamps made in Venice by Alfredo Barbini, Marina Barovia, Archimede Seguso, and the house of Venini. In the entry, a chrome robotic pig lamp from the 1970s with glowing eyes lights the way to two tall French Deco lamps topped with dancing figures by André Arbus. Nearly life-sized stark-white torsos form the bases of a pair of

lamps by James Mont; they sit on a glass table by Donald Desky, who designed the interior of Radio City Music Hall. Graceful wooden lamps from the 1950s by Edward Wormley are nearby. Interspersed among the designer pieces are anonymous lamps that once decorated the living rooms of America—tall, short, boxy, bulbous—some with monstrous chenille shades, with the vivid color combinations (coral and black, dark green and chartreuse) that epitomized the 1950s.

A large showcase near the rear of the store holds hard, boxy Lucite handbags made in the 1940s and '50s. Some are clear, and some are in opaque colors and trimmed with mother-of-pearl or rhinestones. These collectibles can range in price from $200 to $2000. The average price for the handbags at Deco Etc. is about $500.

NEW YORK VINTAGE

117 WEST 25TH STREET

(SIXTH/SEVENTH AVENUES)

☎ 212 647 1107 · *www.newyorkvintage.com*

MON-WED 11AM-6PM; FRI 11AM-6PM;

SAT, SUN 10AM-5PM; CLOSED THU

What to look for: vintage designer evening wear

NEW YORK VINTAGE SELLS COUTURE VINTAGE CLOTHING AND ACCESSORIES, AS WELL AS SMALL personal items such as compacts and cigarette cases. The store has high standards for its collection; store policy is that everything must be of superior quality and in excellent condition. The result is an outstanding shop where the clothing appears to be new—even a peacock blue beaded bustle gown circa 1885. Designers represented include Jean Muir, Mary McFadden, Giorgio Sant'Angelo, Yves Saint-Laurent, and Chanel. Frocks by the avant-

garde master of prints Ossie Clark could be worn, then framed. The selection of evening wear is lovely and affordable. A Gattinoni one-shouldered silk print tea-length cocktail dress from 1972 is $750, and a black taffeta full-skirted floor-length gown with blue velvet trim by Oscar de la Renta is $495. Customers include celebrities, costume designers, stylists, and discerning shoppers looking for that perfect something.

RESTAURANTS

BLUEDOG COFFEE CO.
101 West 25th Street (Sixth/Seventh Avenues)
☎ 212 229 9222 · *www.bluedogcoffeeco.com*
Daily 8:30am-between 4:30 & 6pm

Wonderful coffee, fresh pastries and baked goods, sandwiches, salads, and freshly made entrees that change daily. Limited seating (there is a bench outside). Inexpensive.

CAFÉ AT SHOWPLACE ANTIQUES CENTER
40 West 25th Street (Fifth/Sixth Avenues)
Sat-Sun 8:30am-5:30pm; closed Mon-Fri

Self-service sandwiches, salads, and soft drinks. Inexpensive.

ANTIQUE CAFÉ
55 West 26th Street (at Sixth Avenue)
☎ 212 213 5723
Daily 8am-10pm

Known for seasonal outdoor seating in a sheltered plaza. Serves light breakfasts and lunches, pasta, steak frites, wine, espresso, ice cream. Inexpensive to moderate.

FLEA MARKETS

SHOPS

FLEA MARKETS

ON EVERY SATURDAY AND SUNDAY, WEST 25TH STREET BETWEEN FIFTH AND SEVENTH AVENUES becomes a sprawling market of antiques and collectibles. Itinerant dealers take over a parking lot and a two-story parking garage, complementing permanent antiques shops and cooperatives in the immediate neighborhood.

For almost thirty years the Annex Flea Market set up shop in a nearby parking lot. The Annex was displaced by real estate development, but it has since begun to reappear in the parking lot at the corner of West 17th Street and Sixth Avenue, and on the block of West 39th Street between Ninth and Tenth avenues.

THE ANTIQUES GARAGE

112 WEST 25TH STREET

(SIXTH / SEVENTH AVENUES)

☎ 212 243 5343 · *www.heliskitchenfleamarket.com*

SAT-SUN 6:30AM-5PM; CLOSED MON-FRI

What to look for: general flea-market merchandise;
advertising, prints, photographs, vintage clothing

EVERY WEEKEND THIS PARKING GARAGE BECOMES A FLEA MARKET FREQUENTED BY BROWSERS, collectors, decorators, celebrities, antiques dealers, and bargain hunters. This is the place to search for paintings and prints, vintage clothing and jewelry linens, toys, furniture from many periods, rare books and records, early-twentieth-century glassware and pottery, and New York memorabilia—advertising and ephemera from city businesses, vintage souvenirs, and old photographs of everything from skinny kids playing on stoops to smiling

[162]

prostitutes wearing camisoles and little else. Bargaining is routine, but don't expect the dealer to take more than 25 percent off the asking price. "What is your best price?" is a polite way to begin negotiations.

SHOWPLACE ANTIQUES CENTER

40 WEST 25TH STREET

(FIFTH / SIXTH AVENUES)

☎ 212 633 6063 · *www.nyshowplace.com*

MON-FRI 10AM-6PM; SAT-SUN 8:30AM-5:30PM

What to look for: Judaica, estate jewelry, pottery

THE SPACIOUS FOUR-STORY SHOWPLACE HAS MORE THAN ONE HUNDRED PERMANENT BOOTHS, EACH rented by an independent dealer. Most are open on weekends only, but a new resource, the Showplace on Three, has styled room settings that are open every day with a full staff to answer questions and offer decorating suggestions. The galleries on other floors have high-quality, interesting antiques and collectibles, including Scandinavian and British art pottery, prints and paintings, antique Judaica, Russian icons and silver, Art Deco furniture and accessories, bronze statues, porcelain figurines,

and religious relics. On the first floor, Gallery 41 has old dolls, amateur oil paintings, and nifty vintage sewing items—buttons, fabrics, patterns, notions, pincushions, and unusual tape measures. There is a repair service for silver and other metal objects near the information booth. A café on the lower level is open on weekends and serves sandwiches, sweets, coffee, tea, and soft drinks.

GRAND BAZAAR FLEA MARKET

WEST 25TH STREET

(FIFTH / SIXTH AVENUES)

SAT-SUN 6AM-6PM; CLOSED MON-FRI

What to look for: treasures at bargain prices

Open all year round, the bazaar features eclectic dealers who sell both treasures and trash. Some dealers trade in ethnic items, particularly from Africa and the Middle East, including pottery, statues, textiles, beads, baskets, drums, and small pieces of furniture. Most dealers sell the endless array of flea-market wares. DIY star designers such as Doug Wilson are sometimes seen poking around. There's always a chance of finding something truly special, like an eleven-foot-long Gothic church pew or a passable copy of a Baroque painting.

The formidable 1855 neo-Gothic church that overlooks

the Grand Bazaar Flea Market was originally Trinity Chapel, built as a mid-town branch of Trinity Church. Boss Tweed's daughter was married there in 1877, and Edith Wharton in 1885. Since 1944 it has been St. Sava Serbian Orthodox Cathedral. The church was the target of bombings after the Communist Party established an office at 23 West 25th Street in the early 1960s. It has been neglected and is now under restoration.

ANTIQUE COLLECTIONS INC.

28 WEST 25TH STREET

(FIFTH / SIXTH AVENUES)

☎ 212 367 8808 · *www.antiquecollectionsinc.com*

MON & THU-FRI 11AM-6PM; SAT-SUN 8:30AM-5:30PM;

TUE-WED BY APPOINTMENT

What to look for: a variety of antiques

A FEW DOORS EAST OF THE SHOWPLACE, A DISTINCTIVE INDOOR COOPERATIVE SITS ON THE site of the former home of Lucretia Jones and her daughter Edith Jones Wharton, who lived there from 1882 until her marriage in 1885. Today, antique clothing, textiles, jewelry, and old clocks ticking away in a back corner recall the Gilded Age that Wharton chronicled, and more than one dealer claims to regularly see a ghost that might be her.

To the right of the entrance, William Pass sells couture period clothing of the highest quality at very fair prices. Next to him, Jerome Wilson, Inc., offers pristine Victorian and Edwardian linens, lingerie, and gowns. At the rear, Master Clock restores clocks and watches. Midway on the east side, Illsa Lingerie shows early-twentieth-century lingerie and presents, in a glass case, an informal history of the brassiere.

See the restaurant listings on page 156.

FRESH FLOWERS, PLANTS & FLORAL SUPPLIES

SHOPS

FRESH FLOWERS, PLANTS & FLORAL SUPPLIES

RESTAURANTS

FRESH FLOWERS, PLANTS & FLORAL SUPPLIES

28TH AND 29TH STREETS BETWEEN SIXTH
AND SEVENTH AVENUES

🚇 F, V TO 34TH STREET; 1 TO 28TH STREET

O N 28TH STREET BETWEEN SIXTH AND SEVENTH AVENUES, ON EVERY MORNING EXCEPT SUNday, glory covers grime as foliage and flowers transform the sidewalks into country lanes. Floral designers, event planners, and set decorators rush madly about, music pours out of doorways, and everything smells divine.

Flower dealers have been in this area for more than one hundred years. Cut flowers were a luxury that became available in Manhattan in the mid-nineteenth-century, via growers on Long Island who arrived early every morning by boat to sell to wholesalers and retailers. By 1870 a wholesale flower mart had developed near the docks at the east end of 34th Street. In 1902 the *New York Times* reported that the flower district was relocating to the old Racquet Club Building (later the Coogan Building), at the corner of 26th Street and Sixth Avenue, near their best customers—the theater and hotel district, the shops of Ladies' Mile, and the brothels and nightclubs of the Tenderloin. By 1909 the district extended from Broadway to Seventh Avenue between 24th and 30th Streets. The Coogan Building was demolished in 1999 to make way for an apartment building, effectively displacing the businesses. The current Flower Market is on 28th Street between Sixth and Seventh Avenues, and trickles along Sixth Avenue for a block or two in both directions.

Some merchants, particularly those who deal in cut flowers, sell wholesale only. In this district the interpretation of the rule is loose, meaning that a tax identifica-

[180]

bundles of pussy willows in the spring, sunflowers in the summer, and twining bittersweet in the fall. Arrangements can be ordered from the floral designers on staff, even on short notice.

HOLIDAY FOLIAGE

118 WEST 28TH STREET

(SIXTH/SEVENTH AVENUES)

☎ 212 675 4300

MON-FRI 7AM-6PM; CLOSED SAT-SUN

What to look for: succulents and cacti

THE STAFF AT HOLIDAY FOLIAGE IS EAGER TO DISCUSS THE VARIOUS CACTI AND SUCCULENTS that are its specialty, from large *euphorbia weberbaueri* cacti that almost touch the ceiling to tiny aloe in thimble-sized pots. Tropical potted plants include two hardy houseplant species perfect for offices or neglectful owners—dracaenas, or "corn plants," and snake plants, or "mother-in-laws' tongues"—that are nearly impossible to kill. Snake plants were one of the first houseplants widely sold in the United States, popularized in the 1920s by the Woolworth five-and-ten-cent stores.

[183]

FOLIAGE GARDEN

120 WEST 28TH STREET

(SIXTH/SEVENTH AVENUES)

☎ 212 989 3089 · *www.foliagegarden.com*

MON-SAT 6AM-3PM; CLOSED SUN

What to look for: tropical potted plants and orchids

FOLIAGE GARDEN, WITH ITS DAMP-EARTH AROMAS, IS A JUNGLE-LIKE STORE WITH AN INTERIOR that resembles a set from *King Kong*. Just inside the entrance, rows of shelves hold varieties of orchids, including showy cattleyas and miltonias, spiky-spotted brassias, and leafy cymbidiums, starting at $35. A narrow path leads to the back of the store through exotic potted date and bamboo palms, citrus trees, and jade plants, with neon flowers occasionally emerging from the dense foliage. All plants are grown at the store's greenhouses on Long Island and are very fresh. Three-

[185]

and-a-half-foot potted palms start at $45; price increases with height. Five-foot cone-shaped topiaries of ivy start at $175. Seasonal plants include azaleas and varieties of bromeliads. Ordering can be done on the website, which offers a handy guide for orchid care. There is same-day delivery in the New York metropolitan area weekdays from 7am-5pm. Delivery is also available in the tri-state area at an additional charge.

CARIBBEAN CUTS

120 WEST 28TH STREET

(SIXTH/ SEVENTH AVENUES)

☎ 212 924 6969 · *www.caribbeancuts.com*

MON–FRI 5 30AM-NOON; SAT 6:30AM-11PM;

CLOSED SUN

What to look for: Exotic tropical cut flowers and foliage

EQUATORIAL SUNSHINE SEEMS TO POUR OUT THE DOOR OF THIS STORE, WHICH SELLS FLAMBOY-ant tropical cut flowers and foliage, curiously shaped pods, and entire stalks of bananas, coconut clusters, and bamboo—all imported from the firm's own farms in the Caribbean. Many varieties of ginger are available all year round including regular long-stemmed ginger in varied sizes, Spectabilis "Bee-Hive" Ginger, twisting Costus "Microphone" Ginger, and spectacular but frail Torch Ginger, whose life can be prolonged by spritz-

[188]

ing it with non-stick cooking spray. Delicate purple or white Dancing Ladies are available in the late summer and fall. Unusual species include Octopus Berry, mini-pineapples, and Rhipsalis vine in lengths up to ten feet. The staff whirls back and forth, waiting on the event planners and set decorators who buy here when styling a tropical event or photo shoot, and humming along with the island tunes that play non-stop. The owner is happy to sell to the public, and suggests his exotica for unique parties and weddings. The best days to go are Wednesdays and Saturdays when new shipments arrive. The website has detailed descriptions of species and instructions on their care.

FISCHER & PAGE LTD.

132-134 WEST 28TH STREET

(SIXTH/SEVENTH AVENUES)

☏ 212 645 4106 · *www.fischerandpage.com*

MON-FRI 3:30AM-1:30PM (OR EARLIER);

CLOSED SAT-SUN

*What to look for: cut flowers (at 132); potted topiaries,
orchids, seasonal potted flowers (at 134)*

FISCHER & PAGE OCCUPIES FOUR STOREFRONTS MID-BLOCK ALONG THE SOUTH SIDE OF THE street—one sells cut flowers and adjoins a store for flowering branches, and a double store a few doors west specializes in plants. The cut flower store carries some of the finest to be found in the district—their blossoms grace many of Manhattan's hotels and restaurants and are featured in home decorating magazines. On any day, the selection includes hundreds of different varieties in

[191]

dozens of colors, including roses, tulips, alium, lilacs, hydrangeas, ranunculus, peonies, and lilies, as well as flowering branches and berries. The cut flower and branch divisions do not sell retail, but a business card offered to the cashier is a usually a sufficient credential as long as one is buying an armful and not just a single bouquet. Out-of-town shipping is via air.

Fischer & Page opened its plant shop and seasonal shop next door in 1990. The plant shop is long, narrow, and overgrown with vines, and displays ivy, orchids, bromeliads, rosemary bushes, and more. The adjoining seasonal shop carries Easter lilies, amaryllis, or poinsettias and other seasonal plants. Among the topiaries you might find a three-foot ball-shaped coleus ($35) or a complex spiral ivy globe ($150). Outside are annuals, trays of wheatgrass, and varieties of shrubs and evergreens for rooftop gardens. The store is open to the public; no credentials are required for purchases.

PANY SILK FLOWERS

146 WEST 28TH STREET

(SIXTH/SEVENTH AVENUES)

☎ 212 645 9526

MON-FRI 8AM-5:30PM; SAT 9AM-4PM; CLOSED SUN

What to look for: high-end silk flowers and foliage

PANY SELLS A STAGGERING VARIETY OF HIGH-QUALITY HANDMADE SILK BLOSSOMS, LEAVES, flowering branches, faux fruits and vegetables, and holiday decorations. Stock changes to reflect the seasons, usually every two or three months. A profusion of silk flowers is available, including hydrangeas, water lilies, sunflowers, phlox, irises, poppies, and peonies, as well as oak branches with acorns, pussy willows, and greenery. Custom floral arrangements can be made in any container, including the customer's own, sometimes in as little as two hours. Nonfloral specialties include high-

quality handmade dolls dressed for holidays—witches and pumpkin-head dolls, and snowmen and Santas. Christmas ornaments and beaded branches appear in the store well before Thanksgiving. Prices decrease with quantity purchased.

PLANTER RESOURCE

150 WEST 28TH STREET

(SIXTH/SEVENTH AVENUES)

☎ 212 206 POTS · *www.planterresource.com*

MON-FRI 6AM-3PM; CLOSED SAT-SUN

What to look for: vases and flowerpots

THE MÉLANGE HEAPED ON THE SIDEWALK IN FRONT IS JUST A SAMPLING OF THE IMPRESSIVE selection of pots, vases, and baskets sold at Planter Resource. Containers ranging in size from four inches to more than four feet, made of aluminum, ceramic, zinc, terra-cotta, plastic, wood, and wicker, fill the store almost to the ceiling. Metallic containers in simple and attenuated shapes come in nickel, copper, tin, zinc, and pewter finishes. Lightweight fiberglass urns come in large shapes for decorating stoops and gardens. Terra-cotta pots are round, bell-shaped, square, and rectangu-

lar, many with classical motifs. Glass vases in all sizes and shapes, clear and colored, are sold singly or by the case. A case of seventy-two votive holders costs $72. Potting supplies such as soil and plant stakes are also sold. Many containers are pictured on the website but must be purchased at the store.

STARBRIGHT FLORAL DESIGN

150 WEST 28TH STREET

(SIXTH/SEVENTH AVENUES)

☎ 800 520 8999 · *www.starflor.com*

MON-SAT 8AM-8PM; SUN 9AM-6PM

What to look for: custom floral arrangements

IN A DISTRICT WHERE MANY STORES CLOSE BY 2PM, STARBRIGHT, "THE OFFICIAL FLORIST OF THE CITY that never sleeps," stays open until 8pm. The company's portfolio includes the New York City marathon. From the front of the store, where floral designers build elaborate arrangements, to the rear, where the staff processes orders for gifts ordered on the website, Starbright is filled with cut flowers, bouquets, plants, balloons, and gifts. Orders can be placed online for any type of arrangement.

JAMALI GARDEN SUPPLIES

149 WEST 28TH STREET

(SIXTH/SEVENTH AVENUES)

☎ 212 244 4025 · *www.jamaligarden.com*

MON-SAT 8AM-5:30PM; CLOSED SUN

What to look for: supplies for events, gardening, and floral design

THIS SHOP OFFERS EVERY IMAGINABLE ELEM-ENT FOR FLORAL AND EVENT DESIGN EXCEPT flowers. A small sampling includes pots, potting soil, sand, gravel, twigs, bamboo, glitter sprays, faux autumn leaves, squares of plastic grass, straw matting, Astroturf by the yard, floral lights, lanterns, embroidered and metallic throws, curtain panels, organza in many colors (58 inches by 10 yards for $25), hoses, nozzles, seeds, Christmas garlands, silver-plated urns and candelabra, sticky whitefly traps, wrought-iron hooks, fertilizer,

[201]

floral wire, colored wire, rolls of Mylar, colored tissue paper, corsage pins, hot glue, candlesticks, votive holders, candles, jars of colored sea glass sufficient to fill a medium vase ($10 a jar, six for $48), and Christmas lights year round, as well as cloth, paper, and velvet ribbon. Prices are "semi-retail"—the larger the quantity purchased, the lower the price. Ordering and shipping is available via the website. Orders under $50 are charged a $10 handling fee.

C. C. FLORAL TRADING

139 WEST 28TH STREET

(SIXTH/SEVENTH AVENUES)

☎ 212 594 3870

MON-SAT 9AM-6PM; CLOSED SUN

What to look for: silk garden flowers, especially roses

TALL SHAFTS OF BAMBOO SHADE THE ENTRANCE to tiny C. C. FLORAL TRADING, WHERE EVERY square inch is covered with flowers, hanging vines, and twisting branches—all in silk. While other stores specialize in exotic stems, C. C. has familiar flowers at bargain prices, especially roses in every conceivable color. Interspersed among the tulips, ivy, and pansies are fantasy flora—tiger lilies with petals edged in gold glitter and glitzy silver calla lilies. Shelves hold ribbons, raffia, floral wire, and glue sticks, along with fruits and vegetables. Species rotate with the seasons.

[204]

B & J FLORIST SUPPLY

103 WEST 28TH STREET

(SIXTH/SEVENTH AVENUES)

☎ 212 564 6086

MON-SAT 7AM-5PM; CLOSED SUN

What to look for: ribbon

BUNDLES OF SWEET-SMELLING EUCALYPTUS DYED IN EARTHY TONES, BAMBOO STAKES, AND WICKER baskets in the entryway belie the fanciful party atmosphere inside B & J. There are miles of ribbon—paper, fabric, mesh, solid, plaid, polka-dotted, with and without wired edging. Fabric butterflies with two-foot wingspans dive past oversized artificial apples, oranges, pears, and lemons. Less amusing but useful items are floral wire and tape, adhesives, blocks of Oasis floral foam (for cut flowers) and Dry Oasis (for dried flowers), and a nice assortment of pruning shears and craft scissors.

[205]

RESTAURANTS

IZUMI SUSHI

139 West 28th Street (Sixth Avenue/Seventh Avenue)

☎ 212 273 1169

Mon-Fri 11am-11pm; Sat noon-10:30pm; Sun 5-10:30pm

Popular with locals for fresh sushi. Lunch specials from 11am-4pm. Inexpensive to moderate.

GINGER HOUSE

330 Seventh Avenue (28th/29th Streets)

☎ 212 760 2661

Daily 11am-11pm

Chinese noodle shop and grill bar in comfortable setting. Typical Cantonese and Mandarin dishes include barbecued ribs, duck, and chicken, fresh seafood, and noodle soups. Lunch specials from $4.95. Inexpensive.

SEVEN BAR & GRILL
350 Seventh Avenue (29th/30th Streets)
☎ 212 239 8211 · *www.sevenbarandgrill.com*
Mon-Sat 11:30am-midnight; closed Sun

Sophisticated upscale atmosphere, new American cuisine. Lunch menu includes oysters, homemade ravioli, mac-n-cheese, steak sandwich, varieties of fish, and tapas. Apple martini is recommended. Moderate to expensive.

CHARLESTON'S BISTRO
345 Seventh Avenue (29th/30th Streets)
☎ 212 239 8211
Mon-Fri 7am-7pm, Sat 8am-5pm; closed Sun

Self-service deli. For breakfast, eggs and pastries; for lunch, homemade soups, create-your-own salads and pasta, hot and cold sandwiches, deli specialties. Seating on the mezzanine. Inexpensive to moderate.

THE MILLINERY DISTRICT
BUTTONS, TRIMS & NOTIONS

SHOPS

BUTTONS, TRIMS & NOTIONS

BUTTONS, TRIMS & NOTIONS

I N THE EARLY TWENTIETH CENTURY, WHEN HATS WERE AN ESSENTIAL PART OF APPAREL, THE BLOCKS adjacent to the Garment District from Broadway to Fifth Avenue in the upper Thirties became a center for the wholesale making and selling of hats known as the Millinery District. Architecture followed need, and more than twenty-six new high-rise buildings were built from 1905 to 1930, including the seventeen-story Millinery Towers (1925) on West 37th Street and the twenty-three-story Millinery Building (1927) at 39th and Sixth. Religious needs were met by the Millinery Center Synagogue (1948), which still holds services, on Sixth Avenue between 38th and 39th Streets.

Just before World War II there were almost five hundred millinery-related businesses in the area. Hat manufacturers worked in lofts on upper floors; suppliers provided felt and straw for hat bodies, along with feathers, ribbons, rhinestones, and anything else that could possibly trim a hat. In the 1939 Manhattan Yellow Pages there were forty-four listings under "Rhinestone Goods" alone. including the Eskay Novelty Company, which is still in business but now sells only feathers.

The hat industry began to decline in the 1960s when women started wearing bouffant hairstyles; there is a theory that men stopped wearing hats when John F. Kennedy removed his hat at his inauguration. Although only a few hat manufacturers survive, trimmings stores are still in business, joined by stores selling beads and findings for jewelry making.

DAYTONA BRAIDS & TRIMMINGS

251 WEST 39TH STREET

(SEVENTH/EIGHTH AVENUES)

☎ 212 354 1713

MON-FRI 9AM-5:50PM; SAT 9:30AM-5:20PM;

CLOSED SUN

What to look for: braids, ribbon, lace trimmings

A FAMILY BUSINESS FOR FIFTY-FIVE YEARS, DAY-TONA FORMERLY SOLD TO THE TRADE ONLY, opening to the public fifteen years ago to accommodate the requests of home sewers. The store now ships throughout the United States to individuals, colleges, fashion schools, and small manufacturers, but it has no website and takes orders by telephone only. Racks with spools of ribbon, lace, braid, rickrack, fringe, and embroidered edging stretch for half a block from the entrance; zippers, thread, bias tape, seam binding, and sewing pat-

[213]

terns are less glamorous but useful; there are bushels of buttons. Craft supplies such as embroidery floss, glitter, sequins, and Rit dye are also stocked. The second floor is devoted to supplies for knitting and crocheting.

STEINLAUF & STOLLER

239 WEST 39TH STREET
(SEVENTH/EIGHTH AVENUES)
☎ 212 869 0321 · 877 869 0321
www.steinlaufandstoller.com
MON-FRI 8AM-5:30PM
What to look for: sewing notions

STEINLAUF & STOLLER CARRIES ABSOLUTELY EVERY-THING FOR THE HOME OR PROFESSIONAL SEWER, and it sells both from the midtown store and the website. Some items that are hard to find elsewhere include bra cups for bathing suits and evening wear, dress forms, twenty-five styles of shoulder pads, feather and spiral boning, horsehair up to three inches wide, individual and chain hem weights, pattern drafting tools, bow tie and cummerbund hardware, steel wire for hoop skirts, sewing machine attachments, and a comprehensive

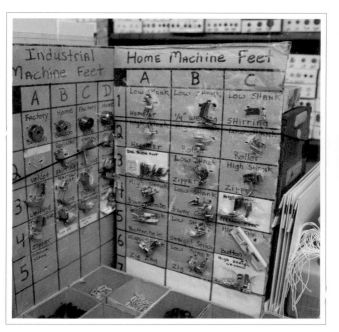

[216]

selection of interfacing, as well woven garments labels (size, care, and fiber content). "Something blue" lace-trimmed bridal garters are $2. Steinlauf & Stoller will ship within a day or two via UPS, there is no minimum order, but orders under $50 require a $5 handling fee.

B & Q BRIDAL

210 WEST 38TH STREET

(SEVENTH/EIGHTH AVENUES)

☎ 212 398 0988

MON-FRI 9:30AM-6:30PM; SAT 10AM-5PM

CLOSED SUN

What to look for: appliqués and beaded fringe

B & Q LOOKS LIKE THE WALK-IN CLOSET OF A WELL-TO-DO DRAG QUEEN. WILDLY COLORFUL FEATHER boas hang above endless bins of beaded tassels, artificial flowers, and intricate handmade appliqués ($1-$10 each). Glittering trims by the yard include beaded fringe (up to five inches long), metallic braid, and sequin rope. A section of bridal headpieces features styles from demure to extreme—pretty pearl headbands with satin rosebuds, rhinestone tiaras with lavender enameled forget-me-nots, gold metallic fabric diadems set with multi-colored jew-

els, and glitzy six-inch-high Miss America–type crowns. "Sweet Fifteen" and "Sweet Sixteen" birthday tiaras are available in pink or blue rhinestones. The store carries plain and beaded veiling to pair with headpieces, provides design advice for the do-it-herself bride, and makes custom headpieces for those less intrepid. Accessories include evening gloves (in white, colors, and above-the-elbow metallic gold), as well as costume jewelry and evening bags.

TOHO SHOJI

990 SIXTH AVENUE (36TH/37TH STREETS)

☎ 212 868 7465 · *www.tohoshojiny.com*

MON-FRI 9AM-7PM; SAT 10AM-6PM;

SUN 10AM-5PM

What to look for: Japanese seed beads

THIS NEW YORK BRANCH OF A TOKYO STORE OFFERS MILLIONS OF JAPANESE SEED BEADS IN every imaginable color packaged in amounts up to one kilogram (105,000 beads). The store also carries a comprehensive selection of glass, wood, bone, ceramic, filigree, and metal beads, as well as pearls and semiprecious stones, chains, rhinestone rope, sterling silver charms, jewelry findings, how-to books, and kits for necklaces and bracelets (with Japanese instructions and English translations). As an official dealer for Swarovski, the store is able to sell the crystals at substantial discounts

[222]

(Swarovski iron-on crystals have just been added to the selection). Many items can be ordered on the website; the minimum order is $50. Large purchases may be eligible for a discount.

M & J TRIMMING

1008 SIXTH AVENUE (37TH/38TH STREETS)

☎ 212 391 6200 · *www.mjtrim.com*

MON-FRI 9AM-7PM; SAT 10AM-5PM; SUN NOON-5PM

What to look for: high-end trimmings

ONE OF LARGEST TRIMMING DISTRIBUTORS IN THE UNITED STATES, M & J BEGAN IN 1936 AS a discount linen store owned by Michael Cohen. In 1959, his son Joel joined the business and began to think about ways to expand. When a visiting salesman asked to borrow five dollars and left a roll of lace as collateral, Cohen quickly sold the lace at a good profit, and, according to family legend, when the salesman returned, shouted, "Forget the five dollars, get me more lace!" Today the three-storefront-wide shop has 20,000-30,000 spools of trimmings, ribbons, and braids; appliqués; buttons; artificial flowers; sequins; rhinestones; and other fine

[225]

embellishments for virtually any project. Unusual items include ostrich feather fringe and safety pins with acrylic tortoise shell Art Deco fasteners. The website is extensive and imaginative, and it includes instructions on how to bejewel a cell phone, iPod, or compact. Even Tiffany & Co. is a customer—its signature gift boxes are tied with ribbon from M & J.

GENUINE TEN TEN

1010 SIXTH AVENUE (37TH/38TH STREETS).
☎ 212 221 1173 · *www.j-genuine.com*
MON-FRI 10AM-7:30PM; SAT-SUN 11AM-6 30PM

What to look for: semiprecious beads

GENUINE TEN TEN SPECIALIZES IN PEARLS AND SEMIPRECIOUS STONE BEADS FROM AROUND THE globe. In chromatic triumph, strings of beads are displayed by color Mauve rhodonite (thirty-three beads for $28) leads to carnelian, then to brick-red jasper. Golden tiger's-eye complements mookaite in variegated earth tones ($20-$60 per string). Contrasting with the stones are freshwater pearls from China, and South Sea pearls from India. Ten Ten will string custom jewelry; delivery time is from ten minutes to one week. Customers are invited to bring a trinket of sentimental value to incorporate into a piece of jewelry. Repair service is also offered.

LOU LOU BUTTONS

69 WEST 38TH STREET (FIFTH/SIXTH AVENUES)

☎ 212 398 5498

MON-FRI 10AM-6:30PM; SAT 1PM-5PM; CLOSED SUN

What to look for: singular handmade buttons

BOTH THE HANDSOME INTERIOR AND THE MERCHANDISE ARE OF NOTE IN THIS NARROW STOREfront, named after a boogeyman in Persian folklore. Many of the buttons are of owner Roz Farhadi's design and are manufactured in Manhattan. The rest are handpicked from manufacturers all over the world. Materials include metal, horn, bone, plastic, glass, ribbon, and coconut shell. Farhadi specializes in manufacturing custom buttons—one, to replace a button lost from a beloved article of clothing, or many, like a six-sided black and silver button with an "Oz" logo for the guards' uniforms in the cast of the Broadway show *Wicked*.

[229]

HYMAN HENDLER & SONS

21 WEST 38TH STREET (FIFTH/SIXTH AVENUES)

☎ 212 840 8393 · *www.hymanhendler.com*

MON-FRI 9AM-5PM; CLOSED SAT-SUN

What to look for: vintage French ribbon

HENDLER, A BUSINESS ESTABLISHED ON A PUSH-CART IN 1900, OPERATED AT 67 WEST 38TH STREET for more than seventy years. The location has changed but the glorious ribbon remains the same. About 75 percent of Hendler's inventory has been manufactured in France from the company's own designs. Over the years orders were received from the French looms and were stacked on shelves in their original boxes wrapped in brown paper. Many are still unopened. The collection is irreplaceable; jacquard ribbons with hand-stuffed trapunto relief designs outlined in metallic threads are the most intricate and valuable. There are delicate silk rib-

[231]

bons with embroidered floral motifs and scalloped edges; wide ribbons that are half velvet and half satin, in contrasting colors; plaid and dotted grosgrain; braided velvets; pale silk moiré with picot edging; and much more. Many ribbons are still purchased in Europe, principally in France or Switzerland, and many are still made to order. The minimum purchase is one-fourth yard.

TINSEL TRADING CO.

47 WEST 38TH STREET

(FIFTH/SIXTH AVENUES)

☎ 212 730 1030 · *www.tinseltrading.com*

MON-FRI 10AM-5:30PM; OCCASIONALLY

SAT 11AM-3PM; CLOSED SUN

*What to look for: antique metallic braids, trims,
and tassels; vintage-inspired gifts*

I N 1933, ARCH BERGOFFEN BOUGHT THE FRENCH
Tinsel Company, where he had worked since
World War I. He renamed his business Tinsel Trading
Company and proceeded to collect gold and silver metallic trimming for five decades. When he died in 1989
his granddaughter Marcia Ceppo adopted the business,
cleaned things up a bit—"it took a case of Murphy's
Oil Soap" for the showcases alone—and continued her
grandfather's calling. The shop, previously dark and

confusing, is luminous and organized. A case of fabulous antique metallic trims is backlit by a photo of Russell Crowe wearing them in *Master and Commander*. Vintage buttons are displayed in an old drawer unit, and an entire wall is devoted to artificial flowers. The store now uses some of its stock of old metallic threads to make items such as tassels and holiday ornaments. New trimmings, appliqués, and ribbons are also sold, along with gifts and decorative seasonal items. Orders can be placed via the website; there is a $75 minimum for shipping.

THE STORE ACROSS THE STREET...

64 WEST 38TH STREET

(FIFTH/SIXTH AVENUES)

☎ 212 354 1242 · *www.tinseltrading.com*

MON-FRI 9:30AM-6PM; OCCASIONALLY

SAT 11AM-4PM; CLOSED SUN

What to look for: vintage ribbon

THE GREAT-GRANDDAUGHTER OF THE FOUNDER OF TINSEL TRADING RUNS THE NEW RIBBON division across the street in the coincidentally named Cinderella Building. The Store Across the Street...carries vintage grosgrain and taffeta ribbons in an abundance of colors and styles, an assortment of new ribbons, including striped grosgrains, ginghams, and plaids, as well as ribbons with floral patterns, and wired ribbons. Small gift items made from ribbon are also sold, including flowers, bracelets, and eyeglass holders.

[237]

ESKAY NOVELTY COMPANY

34 WEST 38TH STREET, THIRD FLOOR

(FIFTH/SIXTH AVENUES)

☎ 212 391 4110 · 800 237 2202

www.eskaynovelty.com

MON-THU 8:30AM-3:30PM; FRI 8:30AM-NOON;

CLOSED SAT-SUN

*What to look for: bouquets of feathers,
feather masks, and boas*

ESKAY IS A TREASURE OF AN OLD NEW YORK BUS-INESS, ONE OF THE LAST STORES IN THE OLD Feather District, adjacent to the Millinery District. Here ladies' hats were once piled with entire iridescent ravens or the wings of pure-white doves. When the elevator door opens on the ground floor of 34 West 38th Street. customers are greeted by the odor of mothballs drifting down from the third floor, where Eskay has been selling

feathers since the late 1940s. Moths adore feathers, but only undyed ones, and the old-fashioned pesticide keeps them out of the bags that fill several large rooms in this old warehouse. In the small showroom, brilliant plumage flutters against peeling gray-green walls, while in the next room steam simmers above a long metal table used for feather fluffing. Professional and amateur designers come here to look for the perfect frippery to trim a coat or a lampshade, or to seek a magnificent feather boa, cape, or stole. You can find a bouquet of fifty peacock plumes, bleached winter-white, or elaborate Mardi Gras masks. Items can be viewed and ordered online; there is no minimum.

MANNY'S MILLINERY
SUPPLY CENTER

26 WEST 38TH STREET

(FIFTH/SIXTH AVENUES)

☎ 212 840 2235

MON-FRI 9AM-5:15PM; SAT 11AM-4PM; CLOSED SUN

What to look for: hatmaking supplies, hatboxes

JUST A FEW DOORS FROM ESKAY IS ANOTHER VES-
TIGE OF THE MILLINERY DISTRICT—MANNY'S,
a reliable standby for theatrical hatmaking. Manny's carries vintage hat blocks, sewing machines, and steam siz-
ers. Supplies include hat frames, brims and crowns, buck-
ram, millinery wire in all weights, straw braid by the
yard, veiling, spray sizing and dyes, glue, feathers, and
trims. The adjoining store carries a new line of waiting-
to-be-trimmed straw and felt hats for both women and
men that can be purchased for DIY decorating. Manny's

has an in-house designer who sees clients by appointment; she can create a hat to match any dress for church or a special occasion, a service that is very popular with mothers of the bride or bridegroom. Manny's can make custom flowers, petals, or leaves from any fabric. Other useful items are hatpins and hatboxes in a range of sizes. The minimum order for shipping is $25.

IN BRIEF

SIL THREAD, INC.
257 West 38th Street
(Seventh/Eighth Avenues)
☎ 212 997 8949
Mon-Fri 8am-6pm; Sat 9am-3pm; Closed Sun

Thread: general-purpose silk, cotton, and cotton wrapped; special-purpose for quilting and leather; waxed for hand sewing; nylon for sergers; rayon for machine embroidery. Dress and upholstery zippers cut to size. Wooden plastic and padded hangers by multipack or case.

TOP TEX TRIMMINGS
222 West 38th Street
(Seventh/Eighth Avenues)
☎ 212 221 6433
Mon-Fri 10am-6pm; Sat 11am-4pm; Closed Sun

Inexpensive passementerie and upholstery trimmings made in China or India. Beaded tiebacks start at $20.

GREAT BUTTONS
1030 Sixth Avenue (38th/39th Streets)
☎ 212 869 6811
Mon-Fri 9am-6pm; Sat 10am-5pm; Closed Sun

Plastic and wood buttons, yarn and knitting supplies, and bridal gowns.

NEW YORK BEADS, INC.
1026 Sixth Avenue (38th/39th Streets)
☎ 212 382 2994
Mon-Fri 9am-6:30pm; Sat-Sun 10am-5pm

Jewelry-making supplies—many, many beads of glass, metal, bone, wood, semiprecious stones; chains; findings; instructional books and videos.

RESTAURANTS

CAFE METRO

530 Seventh Avenue (38th/39th Streets)
☎ 212 398 8788 · *www.cafemetrony.com*
Mon-Fri 7am-7pm; Sat-Sun call for hours

California-casual stop for a quick lunch or snack, offering brick-oven pizza, low-carb lettuce wraps, hot and cold sandwiches, fresh fruit smoothies. There are also salad, pasta, and udon noodle bars. Inexpensive.

STARWICH

72 West 38th Street (Sixth/Fifth Avenues)
☎ 212 302 7775 · *www.starwich.com*
Mon-Fri 7:30am-7pm; Sat-Sun 11am-6pm

Create-your-own sandwich from an imaginative list of organic ingredients (choice of five for $8.95); counter and living room-style seating, wi-fi, and cell phone chargers. Inexpensive.

CROTON RESERVOIR TAVERN
108 West 40th Street
(Sixth Avenue/Broadway)
☎ 212 997 6835 *www.crotonreservoirtavern.com*
Mon.-Wed 11:30am-midnight; Thu-Fri 11:30am-2am;
Sat 2:30pm-2am; closed Sun

A salute to Croton Reservoir, which once occupied the area now covered by the New York Public Library and Bryant Park. American menu of steak and seafood served in an old-style setting includes shrimp cocktail, Cobb salad, steak frites Moderate to expensive.

THE GARMENT DISTRICT
FASHION FABRICS

FASHION FABRICS

RESTAURANTS

SPOSABELLA LACE

252 WEST 40TH STREET
(SEVENTH / EIGHTH AVENUES)
☎ 212 354 4729 · *www.sposabellalace.com*
MON-FRI 9AM-6PM; SAT 9AM-5PM; CLOSED SUN

*What to look for: imported hand-beaded bridal lace,
bridal headpieces*

SPOSABELLA, "BEAUTIFUL BRIDE" IN ITALIAN, SELLS BRIDAL AND EVENING FABRICS AND HEADPIECES at below market prices. Their fabrics and veils have been seen in *W*, *Us*, *Elle Girl*, and *Modern Bride*, and are often used in costumes for film and theater. The store provides yard goods to such top bridal designers as Vera Wang, Amsale, Oscar de la Renta, and Yumi Katsura and sells to the public for the same prices they charge manufacturers. The staff can provide fabrics to replicate almost any gown or veil a bride might wish to copy. Many of

[253]

the fabrics are manufactured abroad for the store, and compare with the supremely high quality textiles used in couture wedding gowns. Sposabella produces their own lace and tulle veiling in France and England, where some of the last of the great lace factories still operate. In the 1940s and '50s most bridal gowns were embellished with lace manufactured in Lyon—Sposabella still contracts with a historic factory there. Fine silk veiling is produced in England on nineteenth century looms; 110-inch-wide lace is $100 per yard. Both lace and veiling are hand-beaded. Many styles of embroidered silk organza appliqués and trims are also stocked.

Custom bridal veils can be ordered; Celine Dion and Whitney Houston had their veils made here. As an alternative, mantillas from Barcelona are $395; custom embroidered mantillas start at $495. Four hundred styles of tiaras and headpieces are stocked, including styles using Swarovski crystal and cubic zirconia. Colored lace and evening fabrics including silk, Duchesse satin, and crystal organza are also available. The website has an extensive product catalog and a directory of recommended wedding-related sites including designers, seamstresses, caterers, florists, cake bakers, photographers. limosine companies, and wedding singers.

N.Y. ELEGANT FABRICS

222 WEST 40TH STREET

(SEVENTH / EIGHTH AVENUES)

☎ 212 302 4984 / 4980 · *www.nyelegant.com*

MON-FRI 9AM-6PM; SAT 10AM-5PM; CLOSED SUN

What to look for: unusual high-end fabrics

ELEGANT FABRICS FROM AROUND THE WORLD FILL EVERY INCH OF THIS SEVENTEEN-THOUSAND-square-foot store. You'll find multicolored pressed felts, hand-dyed raw silks with anodized sequins, Italian linen, European shirting, French wool bouclé, home décor fabrics, beaded brocades reminiscent of Renaissance paintings ($249.95 per yard), French fake fur ($100 per yard), many colors of cotton velvet ($24.95 per yard), and bolt ends at discount. Bolts are displayed so that they can be seen easily; swatches of most fabrics are given freely. The minimum purchase is one-half yard.

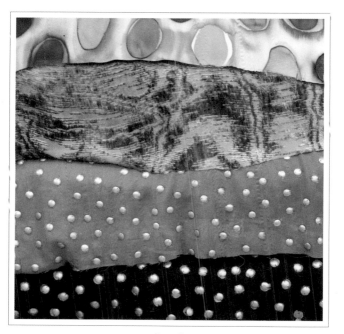

ROSEN & CHADICK FABRICS

561 SEVENTH AVENUE, SECOND AND THIRD FLOORS

(AT 40TH STREET)

☎ 212 869 0142 · *www.rosenandchadickfabrics.com*

MON-FRI 8:30AM-5:45PM; SAT 9AM-4:30PM;

CLOSED SUN

What to look for: cotton and linen

LOCATED IN A BRIGHT CORNER LOFT OVERLOOKING FASHION (SEVENTH) AVENUE, ROSEN & CHADICK carries one the best selections of cotton in the district, including broadcloth and cotton duck. Patterns include designs from the 1940s-1970s, cowboy motifs, and Pop Art illustrations. Linen can be ordered in any of 140 colors at $19.95 per yard; delivery is within two days. Wools include English cashmere suiting, novelty patterns, and textures. Lace, silk, satin, cut velvet, brocade, and specialty theatrical fabric is also stocked.

[259]

BECKENSTEIN FASHION FABRICS

257 WEST 39TH STREET

(SEVENTH / EIGHTH AVENUES)

☎ 212 475 6666 · 800 221 2727

MON-FRI 9AM-5:30PM; SAT 10AM-5:30PM;

CLOSED SUN

What to look for: men's suiting and shirt fabrics

THIS STORE, WHICH SELLS ONLY HIGH-END MEN'S FABRICS, FURNISHED 185 YARDS OF BLACK BAR-athea to make the tuxedoes in the film *Titanic*. Opened by Samuel Beckenstein on the Lower East Side in 1919, there are claims that Beckenstein was the inspiration for the 1932 song "Sam, You Made the Pants Too Long," later sung by Barbra Streisand. Many of the impeccable cashmere, wool, and flannel suitings and cotton shirtings are imported from Europe. Beckenstein is a distributor for the Savile Row company Wain Sheill, and for the

Belgian company Scabal, known for luxury fabrics such as lustrous Diamond Chip suiting made of wool, silk, and diamond fragments; and Gold Treasure, merino wool with twenty-two-carat-gold pinstripes (both priced at $1000 per yard). Made-to-measure shirts and trousers can be ordered; delivery time is about one week.

BUTTERFLY FABRICS

256 WEST 39TH STREET

(SEVENTH / EIGHTH AVENUES)

☎ 212 575 5640 · *www.butterflyfabrics.com*

MON-FRI 9AM-6:15PM; SAT 10AM-5:30PM;

CLOSED SUN

What to look for: discounted imported silk

SOME OF THE MOST SUMPTUOUS FABRICS IN THE DISTRICT CAN BE FOUND AT BUTTERFLY. THE specialty is discounted silk, some of Butterfly's own manufacture and some imported. Colors are luscious, and fabrics include silk organza, dupioni, raw silk, and silk encrusted with beads and sequins. You'll find jewel-toned patchwork; embroidered, striped, or plaid taffeta; multicolor polka dots on a pastel background; beaded and trapunto silk. Prices are competitive; many fabrics start at $35 per yard. At $85 per yard, the hand-beaded

silks are among the most expensive. The store is popular with prominent event and floral designers such as David Stark and Matthew David, as well as fashion and costume designers. The store is sometimes hectic, but the staff provides gracious customer service.

FABRICS GARDEN

250 WEST 39TH STREET

(SEVENTH / EIGHTH AVENUES)

☎ 212 354 6193

MON-FRI 9:30AM-7:30PM; SAT 10AM-7PM;

SUN NOON-5PM

What to look for: fabrics for evening and party gowns;
designer African fabrics

FABRICS GARDEN IS A HOTHOUSE OF EXOTIC YARD GOODS. DIAPHANOUS SILK, NETTING, AND CHIFfon are embellished with silk and sequin flowers. Tiny beads glimmer in the folds of iridescent organza, and pale leaves are appliquéd onto shiny satin. The collection, partly designed in-house, is especially strong on fabrics for wedding gowns and party dresses. Designer fabrics are imported from around the world, many from Brazil, Ecuador, the Dominican Republic, and Santo

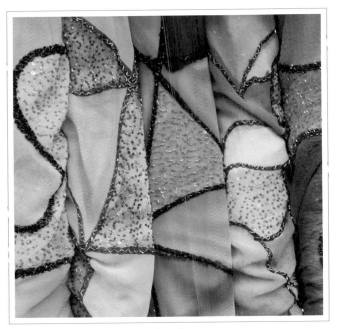

[267]

Domingo. Near the front door are racks of embroidered, beaded, and cutwork fabrics for traditional African dress made by designers from Senegal and Nigeria. The fabrics along the wall to the right of the entrance are discounted evening fabrics acquired from well-known fashion houses; they sell here for $45-$60 per yard. Some bolts from DKNY and Tahari still have original tags. High-quality DKNY denim in assorted colors is $12 per yard. Basic fabrics include raw silk, brocades, printed and solid cottons, cashmere suiting, and fake fur.

LEATHER IMPACT

255 WEST 38TH STREET

(SEVENTH / EIGHTH AVENUES)

☎ 212 302 2332 · *www.leatherimpact.com*

MON-FRI 9:30AM-5:30PM; CLOSED SAT-SUN

What to look for: hides

AN ENTIRE ZEBRA HIDE LIES ACROSS A TABLE BENEATH SHELVES HOLDING STACKS OF FOLDED python and rattlesnake skins, some colored brilliant metallic gold or silver. Hanging nearby, tiny frog skins ($15) might be used for…coasters? With a large selection of exotic skins and more than one hundred colors of dyed lamb leather, Leather Impact is a destination for fashion and costume designers in search of offbeat materials. Natural or dyed cowhide and deerskin are the standbys; ostrich and ostrich leg skins are more unusual. Curiosities include lizard, alligator, shark, and stingray

(the last two are known in processed form as shagreen, used for bookbinding and as veneer for furniture and decorative accessories). Other skins have been embossed, embroidered, stamped with designs, or pierced in overall pattern motifs. Skins are sold by the square foot or the piece. Eccentric trims include realistic-looking barbed wire made of soft leather ($6 per yard). The website has an extensive catalog of swatches; ordering is by phone, fax, or email. Shipping is worldwide.

SPANDEX HOUSE

263 WEST 38TH STREET

(SEVENTH / EIGHTH AVENUES)

☎ 212 354 6711 · *www.spandexhouse.com*

MON-FRI 9AM-6PM; SAT 10AM-5PM; CLOSED SUN

What to look for: everything stretch

AT SPANDEX HOUSE EVERYTHING STRETCHES, INCLUDING THE PRICES. THE STORE CARRIES one of the largest selections of spandex and Lycra in the world, with eighteen thousand square feet of stretch on four levels. Fabrics include wet-look spandex, slinky glitter mesh, big-hole fishnet, and power net. Stretch holograms come in solids, metallics, animal prints, and tie-dyes. Uses include costumes for theater, cinema, dance, wrestling, burlesque, and circus acts, as well as uniforms for sports and cheerleading. Swimwear and foundation garment manufacturers are faithful customers. Testi-

[273]

monials are posted everywhere, with photos and auto-graphed posters from skater Oksana Baiul, Charlie's Angels, and Spiderman. Spandex House has a huge mail-order and internet business, with more than eight thousand accounts, including schools, universities, and the U.S. Roller Skating Team. Hundreds of samples are pictured on the website; there is a ten-yard minimum for mail orders. Sampler "value packs" totaling twenty-five yards of assorted colors or patterns are $50-$125.

MOOD DESIGNER FABRICS

255 WEST 37TH STREET, THIRD FLOOR

(SEVENTH / EIGHTH AVENUES)

☎ 212 730 5003 · *www.moodfabric.com*

MON-FRI 9AM-7PM; SAT 10AM-4PM; CLOSED SUN

What to look for: closeout designer fabrics

DESIGNER CLOSEOUT FABRICS FROM FASHION HOUSES SUCH AS MARC JACOBS, CALVIN KLEIN, and Donna Karan are one reason for the popularity of this busy store, frequented by costumers, quilters, mothers-of-the-bride, and designers. A dizzying array of wool, satin, denim, taffeta, vinyl, velvet, and flannel, along with less familiar ones, such as cloque, marquisette, sendal, moreen, camlet, and grenadine, are displayed in the huge sales loft. Complimentary swatches are provided in the store, by phone request, or via the website. One-quarter yard is the minimum for cut yardage.

IN BRIEF

PARON FABRICS WEST AND PARON ANNEX
206 West 40th Street
(Seventh/Eighth Avenues)
☎ 212 768 3266 · *www.paronfabrics.com*
Mon-Fri 9am-5pm; Thu 9am-7pm;
Sat 9am-5pm; Closed Sun

Large assortment of wool suiting, wool checks, and plaids. At the Annex, everything is 50 percent off the lowest price.

AYAZMOON FABRIC
214 West 39th Street
(Seventh/Eighth Avenues)
☎ 212 869 3315
Mon-Fri 9am-7pm; Sat 10am-6pm; Sun 11am-5pm

Chinese brocade and embroidery, and Indian sari fabrics.

RESTAURANTS

DJERDAN RESTAURANT

221 West 38th Street (Seventh/Eighth Avenues)
☎ 212 921 1183
Mon 11am-7pm; Tue-Fri 11am-10pm;
Sat 12-10 pm; Sun noon-7 pm

This Balkan restaurant serves homemade ethnic dishes.

BEN'S DELICATESSEN

209 West 38th Street (Seventh/Eighth Avenues)
☎ 212 398 2367 · *www.bensdeli.net*
Daily 11am-9pm

Restaurant serving delicatessen fare, and more. Moderate.

ARNO RISTORANTE

141 West 38th Street (Broadway/Seventh Avenue)
☎ 212 944 7420 · *www.arnoristorante.com*
Mon-Fri 11:45am-10pm; Sat 4-10pm; closed Sun

Elegant restaurant serving typical Italian dishes. Expensive.

THE DIAMOND DISTRICT
JEWELRY

THE DIAMOND DISTRICT
JEWELRY

THE DIAMOND DISTRICT
JEWELRY
WEST 47TH STREET BETWEEN FIFTH
AND SIXTH AVENUES

🚇 B, D, F, V TO 47TH-50TH STREETS/
ROCKEFELLER CENTER

AROUND 1840, DIAMOND DEALERS SETTLED IN LOWER MANHATTAN ON MAIDEN LANE NEAR Wall Street, where they catered to the carriage trade for a century. When World War II fueled a boom on Wall Street, downtown rents escalated and jewelers moved uptown in search of cheaper quarters. They settled on 47th Street between Fifth and Sixth Avenues, where the rag business was about to be rendered obsolete by the advent of paper towels. Close to the modern carriage trades of both Fifth Avenue and the theater district, the area was ideal for diamond merchants.

[280]

After the war, jewelers from Europe, especially the diamond centers of Amsterdam and Antwerp, immigrated to America and set up shop on 47th Street, joining the jewelers who were already there. Since then, waves of displaced jewelers from around the world have moved to 47th Street, setting up booths in the jewelry exchanges or simply trading on the street. It is said that fashion trends in jewelry begin on 47th Street, influenced by the ethnicity of the most recently arrived jewelers.

By 1970, the diamond business had taken over every storefront on the south side of the street and 80 percent of those on the north side. There are now more than twenty-six hundred independent diamond-related businesses on the block. The proximity of traders, craftsmen, and dealers makes it possible for jewelers to offer an array of merchandise and services equaled only by the markets in Antwerp and South Africa.

Shoppers should note that, in general, the closer the

store is to Fifth Avenue, the higher the prices. Individual jewelers rent small booths in large mall-like spaces called exchanges; each exchange has its own character.

Established in 1947, the National Jewelers Exchange at 4 West 47th Street is one of the oldest, with many longtime merchants who have reputations of being both experienced and ethical. Slightly removed from Fifth Avenue, it has a comfortable, low-pressure atmosphere. On the mezzanine, the Diamond Dairy Restaurant overlooks the trading floor like a sort of observation deck; one can enjoy kosher home cooking while surveying the action below.

Current contemporary jewelry designs can be found at the exchange at 13 West 47th Street, while the exchange at 36 West 47th Street, the Diamond Center of America, is known for estate jewelry. This is where costume designers for film and advertising go to rent jewels. You may see some dealers sitting, mysteriously, behind empty cases—this means that all their pieces are cut on loan. The World's Largest Jewelry Exchange, at 55 West 47th Street, has five hundred booths and a beauty salon that specializes in Russian hairstyles.

Keep in mind that booths with window displays pay the highest rent—when looking for bargains, venture into the interior of the exchange. The businesses in the very back are often wholesale only. Most businesses on the upper floors of buildings are not retail establishments.

When buying a loose diamond it is highly recommended to select one that has been examined, graded, and certified by either the Gemological Institute of America (GIA) or the American Gem Society (AGS). There are other labs, but these are the most widely known and respected. The diamond's certificate will be issued with the stone. All diamonds weighing more than 1.5 carats must be certified; if purchasing a smaller stone that has no certificate, insist that the jeweler write all properties attributed to it on the receipt. This is, in effect, a written guarantee in case the stone proves to be other than what it was represented as being.

Don't buy the first piece you see, and don't buy from, or sell to, vendors on the street. Don't be swayed by pushy dealers; continue to shop until you feel comfortable. As one venerable jeweler put it, "Trust your instincts. If it seems too good to be true, it is."

The district has an excellent website, www.47th-street.com. A tour of the district every Wednesday morning at 9:30 covers history, architecture, and the rudiments of shopping for jewelry, diamonds, and gemstones. Reservations can be made at babylon@pipeline.com or by calling (212) 398-3087. The tour lasts about an hour and costs $10.

ERIC ORIGINALS & ANTIQUES LTD.

National Jewelers Exchange

4 WEST 47TH STREET, BOOTHS 2-3

(FIFTH/SIXTH AVENUES)

☎ 212 819 9595

MON-FRI 10AM-5PM; CLOSED SAT-SUN

What to look for: antique and vintage diamond jewelry

THE $48,000 SIGNED TIFFANY ART DECO BRACELET LYING CASUALLY ON THE GLASS COUNTERTOP is one example of the rare pieces, from the eighteenth century to the 1940s, to be found here. There are antique pieces from Cartier and other legendary houses, some still in their original boxes. A magnificent Van Cleef & Arpels necklace, circa 1920s, with the French mark, has forty-five carats of round diamonds in sizes graduated from one to five carats, and accented by forty carats of

baguette diamonds. It sells for just under one million dollars. In the window, heavy gold chairs and strings of enormous pearls encircle a strange tiara made of little diamond men. An unusual pin, of crossed platinum feathers, enameled in soft colors and set with diamonds, draws attention, and two large bumblebee brooches sparkle in the late afternoon sunlight. A few new pieces are also sold.

1,873 UNUSUAL WEDDING RINGS

National Jewelers Exchange

4 WEST 47TH STREET, BOOTH 86

(FIFTH/SIXTH AVENUES)

☎ 212 944 1713 · 800 877 3874

www.unusualweddingrings.com

MON-FRI 10AM-5PM; CLOSED SAT-SUN

What to look for: wedding rings

HERE YOU'LL FIND MANY MORE THAN 1,873 RINGS FOR BOTH MEN AND WOMEN. THERE ARE ONE-of-a-kind vintage and antique rings; Celtic rings; rings made from silver, gold, platinum, enamel, titanium, and tungsten; plain bands and bands set with diamonds, jewels, pearls, or semiprecious stones. Rings can be designed to customers' specifications and can incorporate diamonds or gold from old family rings. Custom rings also can be produced overnight for ardent couples (many of

[289]

whom are tourists who decide impulsively to get married in New York City). The owner also claims that he does a brisk business in replacements for men who have lost their wedding bands. Rings can be custom ordered via the website or by telephone. There is a ten-day return policy.

The owner, Herman Rotenberg, is profoundly knowledgeable about the district and enjoys being an unofficial tour guide. He will generously refer you to other reputable jewelers and services.

JAMIE LERMAN INC. /
SANDY STEVEN ENGRAVERS

National Jewelers Exchange

4 WEST 47TH STREET, BOOTH 84

(FIFTH/SIXTH AVENUES)

☎ 212 921 5976 · *www.sandystevenengravers.com*

MON-FRI 10AM-5PM; CLOSED SAT-SUN

What to look for: engraving

MASTER ENGRAVER JAMIE LERMAN ETCHES ON PRACTICALLY ANYTHING—GOLD, SILVER, PLATinum, glass, Lucite, toaster ovens, golf clubs, and iPods. He personalizes wedding bands (his favorite inscriptions include "Put me back on" and "Mess around—die"). Engraving is done by hand, computer, machine, or laser. One-day or while-you-wait service is possible; text can be in any language. Engraved corporate gifts are a specialty.

EUGENE KOROBOK

National Jewelers Exchange

8 WEST 47TH STREET, BOOTH 55

(FIFTH/SIXTH AVENUES)

☎ 212 354 4795

MON-THU 11AM-5PM; FRI 11AM-2PM;

CLOSED SAT-SUN

What to look for: repairs

IN THE MIDST OF A JUMBLE ACCUMULATED OVER THIRTY YEARS, EUGENE KOROBOK REMAKES JEWelry to specification, sizes rings, resets lost stones, and fixes clasps. He is a ninth-generation jeweler. His counter is filled with antique tools that have been in his family for more than 150 years, including a mold for hammering silver to adorn the hilts of swords. Korobok will not bargain—the prominent "Repairs" sign on his counter reads, "I am NOT a non-profit organization."

LEIGH JAY NACHT

New York Jewelry Center

10 WEST 47TH STREET, BOOTH 10

(FIFTH/SIXTH AVENUES)

☎ 212 719 2888 · *www.antiqueengagementrings.com*

TYPICALLY MON-THU 10AM-5PM; FRI 10AM-3PM;

CLOSED SAT-SUN; CALL FOR APPOINTMENT

What to look for: Edwardian and Art Deco
engagement rings

E VEN DEVOTEES OF MODERN DESIGN WILL APPRE-
CIATE THE BEAUTY OF THE NINETEENTH- AND
early-twentieth-century engagement rings that fill the
case at this booth. Art Deco rings, crafted during the
Depression when labor and diamonds were inexpensive,
are especially lovely. Vintage diamonds, lit with what
Nacht describes as "brilliance that is kaleidoscopic," are
entwined in intricate filigree settings. Antique pieces are

becoming rare, so Nacht reproduces antique rings and settings that are hard to differentiate from the originals. He also carries wedding bands; most of his collection is for women, but he does carry a few men's rings. An extensive website pictures many of the rings, which can be ordered online or by telephone. There is a thirty-day money-back guarantee. Sizing and shipping are free.

GRAY & DAVIS, D.K. BRESSLER

32 WEST 47TH STREET, BOOTH 1 AND 3

(FIFTH/SIXTH AVENUES)

☎ 212 719 4698 · 212 302 2177

MON-FRI 10:30AM-5:30PM; CLOSED SAT-SUN

What to look for: antique jewelry

GRAY BOONE AND RONALD KAWITZKY, WELL KNOWN AMONG THE COGNOSCENTI FOR THEIR estate jewelry, preside each weekday at neighboring booths that contains some of the most exquisite pieces on the street, many of which are surprisingly affordable. Nineteenth century Italian micro-mosaic brooches with cherubs or scenes of the Roman Forum are displayed alongside earbobs of pietra dura (Italian hard stone), carved coral, gutta percha (early hard rubber), and gold set with hand-carved cameos. Their offerings might include such rarities as an incised golden locket shaped like a cube that folds apart to reveal a tiny round portrait of a child on each side, or an eighteenth-century mourning ring inscribed to the memory of a long dead member of Parliament. Many pieces are Etruscan Revival attributed to, or inspired by, the designs of the Castellani Brothers, whose firm in Rome opened in 1814, and was an obligatory stop for travelers taking the Grand Tour. Boone explains that these old pieces were possible to make because although Victorian gold was expensive, craftsmanship was cheap—the exact opposite of today.

NORMAN LANDSBERG

66 WEST 47TH STREET, BOOTH 66

(FIFTH/SIXTH AVENUES)

☎ 212 391 1980 · *www.normanlandsberg.com*

MON-FRI 10AM-5PM; SAT 10AM-5PM; CLOSED SUN

*What to look for: discounted jewelry by
contemporary designers*

Unlike many merchants on the street, Norman Landsberg in a native New Yorker, born and raised in the Bronx. His booth is a hub of action as he, his two sons, and five sales assistants answer the clamoring phone and wait on a stream of customers, some of whom who have been buying from them since the firm was founded fifty-seven years ago. Diamond necklaces, bracelets, earrings, and brooches, as well as engagement, wedding, and cocktail rings radiate fire from the cases; many are by contemporary designers such as Jeff Cooper, Christian Bauer, Martin Flyer, and Daniel K, who are sold on 47th Street only at Landsberg. The dealer also carries a large selection of GIA-certified loose diamonds and will quote prices in person or via the website, which also has a useful page showing the properties of diamonds and how they are graded. For novices, an appointment can be made with one of the staff for an individual session on how to buy a diamond.

LEON ZOLAND & SON

75 WEST 47TH STREET (FIFTH / SIXTH AVENUES)
☎ 212 575 8890 · *www.zolands.com*
MON-FRI 10AM-5PM; SAT 10AM-4:30PM;
CLOSED SUN

What to look for: GIA-certified diamonds, loose stones

The Zolands run a four-generation family business that is more than seventy-five years old and was one of the first diamond businesses to locate on 47th Street. The building they own, located near Sixth Avenue with corresponding lower prices, contains a small diamond and jewelry exchange. Their booth is situated in the flagship position, with a window that glitters with thousands of stones set in engagement and wedding rings, necklaces, bracelets, pins, and earrings. A six-carat pear-shaped diamond engagement ring, a bracelet of marquise-cut diamonds by Kurt Gaum,

[303]

Italian white gold earrings with cabochon sapphires, and a heart-shaped pendant with more than fifty diamonds are typical stock. The firm deals in GIA-certified diamonds and has loose stones for many uses. Diamonds and other jewelry are bought from individuals by appointment. Some items are pictured on the website. There is a seven-day return policy for noncustomized items. Along with GIA certificates, an appraisal will be issued for insurance purposes. Shipping via registered, insured mail is free of charge.

RUDLIER JEWELRY

15 WEST 47, BOOTH 42 (FIFTH/SIXTH AVENUES)

☎ 212 354 1733

MON-FRI 10AM-5PM; CLOSED SAT-SUN

What to look for: handcrafted jewelry
influenced by Fabergé

VICTORIA RUDLÉ SELLS JEWELRY MADE BY HER FATHER, SIMON, A THIRD-GENERATION JEWELER who, like his father and grandfather, worked in the Moscow studio of the great firm of Fabergé. It is difficult for a layman to tell the difference between the work done by Mr. Rudlé and the original Fabergé pieces. On display are enameled eggs that shelter tiny ballerinas, a box with the picture of the tsar-heir Alexander, and miniature baskets of flowers set with jewels. Exquisite pins en tremblant, an almost forgotten style that was popular in France one hundred years ago, are constructed with tiny

[306]

springs that allow the gems to move and sparkle. Rudlier also specializes in custom work, furnishing the stones or using those of the client. Many customers are Europeans who appreciate the historic foundations of the firm's work. Prices can top $200,000, but there are items starting at $800.

IN BRIEF

AA PEARL & GEM
New York Jewelry Center
10 West 47th Street, Booth 5
(Fifth/Sixth Avenues)
☎ 212 869 2883 · *www.aapearlny.com*
Mon-Fri 9am-5pm; Closed Sat-Sun
What to look for: pearl stringing

Loose imported cultured pearls from Australia, Tahiti, Indonesia; Akoya pearls from Japan; mabe and freshwater varieties; repairs, stringing, and restringing of pearls and semiprecious stone beads; diamond and pearl clasps are available for custom necklaces.

HOWARD FASS AT PACCICO & PACCICO
The Diamond Horseshoe
29 West 47th Street, Mezzanine No. 5
(Fifth/Sixth Avenues)
☎ 212 382 0779
Mon-Thu 9am-5pm; Fri 9am-noon;
Closed Sat-Sun

Expert watch repairs by president of the Horological Society of New York.

STEVE'S JEWELRY CO.
Futurama Diamond Exchange
66 West 47th Street, Mezzanine No. 14
(Fifth/Sixth Avenues)
☎ 212 354 1291
Mon-Fri 10:30am-5:30pm ("sometimes"); closed Sat-Sun

Complete remodeling and restoration. Rings sized, clasps fixed, general jewelry repairs.

RESTAURANTS

DIAMOND DAIRY OF NEW YORK
4 West 47th Street (Fifth/Sixth Avenues)
☎ 212 719 2694
Mon-Thu 7:45am-4:45pm; Fri 7:30am-2:00pm;
closed Sat-Sun

Kosher dairy restaurant on the mezzanine of the National Diamond
Exchange with fabulous cheese blintzes and a view of the action
below. Serves homemade dishes for breakfast and lunch, omelettes,
vegetable soup, *cholent* baked beans, stuffed cabbage, and chow
mein. Inexpensive.

BERGER'S DELICATESSEN
44 West 47th Street (Fifth/Sixth Avenues)
☎ 212 719 4173
Mon-Fri 6am-7pm; Sat 7am-5pm; closed Sun

Boisterous delicatessen with huge sandwiches served with a pickle
and all the mustard you can eat. Egg creams are seductively old-
fashioned. Inexpensive.

DISTRICT RESTAURANT AND THE MINI-BAR
THE MUSE HOTEL
130 West 46th Street (Sixth/Seventh Avenues)
☎ 212 485 2400 · 877 NYC-MUSE · *www.themusehotel.com*
District Restaurant: Mon-Fri breakfast 6:30am-10:30am; lunch noon-
2pm; Mon-Sat pre-theatre 5pm-6:30pm; dinner 7pm-10pm;
Sat-Sun breakfast 7am-11am
Mini-Bar: Mon-Fri noon-midnight; Sat-Sun 4pm-midnight

In the cozy Mini-Bar drinks, mini burgers, and snacks; for lunch,
wilted spinach and warm lobster salad, spicy buffalo wing "lolli-
pops," thin-crust pizza sandwiches, burgers. Moderate to expensive.

LE MARAIS
150 West 46th Street (Sixth/Seventh Avenues)
☎ 212 869 0900 · *www. lemarais.net*
Sun-Thur noon-midnight (Sun brunch noon-3pm);
Fri noon-2:30pm; Sat sundown-1am

French steakhouse serving cuts of beef and veal, duck, chicken,
whole fish of the day, salads, french fries, profiteroles, chocolate
mousse. Sunday brunch noon to 3pm. Moderate to expensive.

MUSICAL INSTRUMENTS

MUSICAL INSTRUMENTS

46TH TO 48TH STREETS FROM

SIXTH AVENUE TO BROADWAY

🚇 B, D, F, V TO 47-50TH

STREETS / ROCKEFELLER CENTER

THESE BLOCKS, LINED WITH MUSICAL INSTRU-MENT STORES, HAVE LONG BEEN DEVOTED TO the music profession. According to the 1939 *WPA Guide to New York City*, "At about four o'clock every afternoon the swing musicians gather on the west side of Broadway near Forty-eighth Street to gossip and to exchange ideas for new variations in hot music."

In the early decades of the twentieth century, when the Times Square theater district was young and growing, orchestra and jazz rehearsal spaces sprang up in the upper stories along West 48th Street. Musicians were drawn to the block by the studios, and by Jim and Andy's Bar at the east end of the block. Jim and Andy's was a combination green room and union hall—clubs and orchestras called the bar with requests for musicians, and whoever was hanging around and fit the bill got the job. Meanwhile, music teachers who gave classes on the block provided instruments for those who had none, and they soon began to sell them, prompting the opening of musical instrument stores. The block became internationally known as Music Row, where musicians could find emotional, creative, financial, and physical sustenance.

In the 1950s and early '60s there were twenty-four shops on the block supporting not only theater and concert musicians but also pop and rock performers. Some worked around the corner at 1619 Broadway in the Brill Building, a one-stop composing, recording, and publishing headquarters. A generation of American teenagers adored the "Brill Building sound," of singer/songwriters such as Bobby Darin, Neil Sedaka, and his high-school girlfriend Carole King, who wrote songs such as "Stupid Cupid," "Splish-Splash," "Calendar Girl," "Will You Still Love Me Tomorrow," and "Up on the Roof."

In the mid-1960s Rockefeller Center bit into the east end of the block, displacing Jim and Andy's and several longtime stores. Some stores moved to 46th Street, where they remain today. Later the chain Sam Ash bought out other independent dealers. The few who survive are true veterans of American music history.

NEW YORK WOODWIND
AND BRASS

168 WEST 48TH STREET

(SIXTH / SEVENTH AVENUES)

☎ 212 302 5893

MON-SAT 10AM-6PM; SUN 11AM-5PM

What to look for: vintage brass and
woodwind instruments

W HEN THE WARSAW SYMPHONY, RUSSIAN PHIL-
HARMONIC, OR ROYAL CONCERTGEBOUW ORCH-
estra is in town, the musicians consider New York
Woodwind and Brass a mandatory stop. Founder Rod
Baltimore has been working on the block for fifty-seven
years, since he was twelve years old To earn money for
music lessons he shined the shoes of musicians at Jim
and Andy's Bar, drumming up business by crawling
around on the floor and tapping guys on the feet. He

[318]

studied instrument repair in Europe and then worked for another music store legend, Charlie Ponte, before opening his own store. In addition to buying and selling instruments, Baltimore will restore and/or appraise antique and vintage instruments. He also rents them as props and sells them to amateur and professional interior designers for their decorative value.

ALEX MUSICAL INSTRUMENTS, INC.

165 WEST 48TH STREET, SECOND AND THIRD
FLOORS (SIXTH/SEVENTH AVENUES)

☎ 212 819 0070 · *www.alexmusicalinstruments.com*

MON-FRI 10AM-5:30PM; SAT 10AM-5PM;

CLOSED SUN

What to look for: accordions

A CACOPHONY OF LAUGHTER, CHATTER IN SEVERAL LANGUAGES, AND THE DISTINCTIVE WHEEZY carnival music of accordions coming down the stairwell leads visitors to Alex Carozza's third-floor showroom, where he sells new and vintage accordions. Accordions may be low visibility for most, but according to Carozza they are essential to more than one hundred Mexican bands in New York City alone. New accordions range from $700 to $3000. The store also has a repair service that,

[321]

in addition to repairing accordions, also restores guitars, banjos, and other stringed instruments. On the second floor Carozza has created a small museum built around his collection of antique accordions. The highlight is a 1926 New York-made accordion in mint condition, decorated with jeweled mermaids, that Carozza enjoys demonstrating. It still plays like the day it was made.

RUDY'S MUSIC STOP

169 WEST 48TH STREET

(SIXTH/SEVENTH AVENUES)

☎ 212 391 1699 · *www.rudysmusic.com*

MON-SAT 10:30AM-7PM; CLOSED SUN

What to look for: guitars

WHEN RUDY PENSA LEFT HIS NATIVE ARGEN-
TINA HE SAYS IT WASN'T TO GO TO NEW YORK,
it was to go to 48th Street. He started building guitars
when he was thirteen, studied classical guitar, fell in love
with the Beatles, and opened his store on Music Row in
1978. His first custom-built guitar, the R Custom, was
introduced in 1982. His most famous is the now-classic
Pensa MK1, which was designed with Mark Knopfler of
the band Dire Straights. The Pensa MK2 was introduced
in 2000.

New and vintage electric guitars and amplifiers are

displayed on the first floor, with new acoustic guitars, banjos, mandolins, and ukuleles on the second. The third floor is devoted to basses, and the fourth floor houses vintage and antique acoustic guitars. Guitar straps, picks, accessories, and a wide selection of strings are also sold.

Worldwide shipping is available. There is a twenty-four-hour approval period on instruments; amplifiers cannot be returned. Experts will appraise guitars and basses in the store or from photographs, and issue written evaluations. Appraisals are $30. Daily and weekly rentals of instruments are available.

COLONY MUSIC CENTER

1619 BROADWAY (AT 49TH STREET)

☎ 212 265 2050 · *www.colonymusic.com*

MON-SAT 9:30AM-1AM; SUN 10AM-MIDNIGHT

What to look for: music collectibles and karaoke CDs

IN A CORNER OF THE BRILL BUILDING THE MUSIC TRADITION CONTINUES AT SLIGHTLY FUNKY AND fabulous Colony Music. Behind golden doors with treble clefs for handles, performers peruse the enormous selection of sheet music and scores, both new and old, for the perfect audition material. Colony also has a comprehensive selection of CDs from Broadway shows.

Glass cases lining the back walls are filled with memorabilia from music, theater, film, and television. The collections are so extensive that a full-time curator is employed to maintain them. All the items are for sale. Some cases are devoted to individual entertainers;

the Beatles and Elvis Presley each have two. Another is given to *I Love Lucy*, and yet another contains a comprehensive collection of *TV Guide* magazines. Barbra Streisand and Judy Garland are represented, as is Madonna. The Frank Sinatra case contains programs, tickets, sheet music, buttons, medals, and commemorative plates spanning his entire career.

Colony claims it offers the world's largest selection of karaoke CDs and equipment. No longer do aspiring singers have to take a piano accompanist to auditions; it's all done with karaoke. Subway musicians, too, benefit from the selection.

Many items can be ordered via the website. Orders received before 4pm are usually shipped the same day.

DRUMMER'S WORLD

151 WEST 46TH STREET, THIRD FLOOR

(FIFTH / SIXTH AVENUES)

☎ 212 840 3057 · *www.drummersworld.com*

MON-FRI 10AM-6PM; SAT 10AM-4PM; CLOSED SUN

What to look for: unusual percussion instruments

D RUMMER'S WORLD CLAIMS TO BE THE FIRST
STORE IN NEW YORK CITY TO OFFER AN EXTENS-
ive range of instruments used in international and indig-
enous percussion. World instruments include African
caxixi and talking drums, Nigerian log drums, Chilean
goat toe shakers, Brazilian *pandeiros,* and *doumbeks* from
the Middle East. Endemic to the United Sates, the Thun-
derecho Trash Kat is made from a galvanized trash can;
the Cajun rub-board, or *frattoir,* is worn on the chest and
played with spoon handles or thimbles. Classical percussion instruments sold at Drummer's World include snare

drums, chimes, triangles, cymbals, and castanets.

The store carries many brands of drums, as well as its own line of drum sets, including one for collectors made from American burl maple ($4,400) and a set of nesting drums designed for portability. Thousands of drumsticks are stored in cubbyholes behind the counter. An in-house shop does repairs, recovering, and customizing, and specializes in mounting head skins on bongos, congas, frame drums, ashikos, djembes, and tambourines. Orders can be placed via the website but returns are not accepted; shipping is extra.

See the restaurant listings on page 310.

AUTHOR'S FAVORITES

INDEX

NOTES

NOTES

NOTES

NOTES

NOTES

NOTES

NOTES

NOTES

NOTES

NOTES

NOTES

NOTES

NOTES

NOTES